PRAISE FOR THIS B

"Plugs you into the energy

"Shelley and Ormond are fantastic teachers who take you on a journey through the exotic inner landscape of your mind. You'll learn tools that capture what you need to create your ultimate reality and dreams."
Shelby Harris, C.Ht.
Hypnotherapist/Healer

"Simple practices that reveal beauty and meaning in your life."
Josan Galletti,C.Ht.
Author, *Primer to the Light:
A Spiritual Book For Everyone*

"This book gave me the insight, clarity, vision and tools to reach my most precious moments and to help others do the same. It is an honor to spend an evening with Ormond and Shelley."
Carol Lischka Orlick

"A wake up call for your soul. When these thoughts walk through your mind, the door to higher consciousness opens."
Lynn Morgan Loa,
Television Producer

"You'll never see the world the same way again."
Joan Meijer-Hirschland
Author, *Tranquillity Initiative*

"This book wipes clean the slate of convoluted thinking and I begin with a fresh awareness. Stockwell and McGill took me by the hand and said; 'You are not alone. Come with me…you are luminous.'"
Nica Lee
Editing Consultant

"Sit back, awaken your heart, allow your mind to expand and experience the power of your highest self. Ormond and Shelley open the gates of unconditional love. Thank you for helping me to touch my soul."
Suzy Prudden, C.Ht.
Author, *Suzy Prudden's Take Two
Minutes to Save Your Life*

Also Available from Creativity Unlimited Press

BOOKS
Automatic Writing and Heiroscripting: Tap Unlimited Creativity and Guidance
Channeling: You Conduit!
Denial is Not a River in Egypt: Stockwell's Hypnosis System to Life's Promised Land
Everything You Ever Wanted to Know about Everything
Hypnosis: How to Put a Smile on Your Face and Money in Your Pocket
Insides Out: Self-Talk Poetry
Sex and Other Touchy Subjects: Transformational Poetry
Stockwell's Hypnosis for Weight Loss: 10 Easy Steps to a New You
The Search for Cosmic Consciousness: The Hypnosis Book Einstein Would Have Loved
The Secrets of Hypnotizing Men
The Secrets of Hypnotizing Women
Time Travel: The Do-It-Yourself Past Life Journey Handbook

AUDIOTAPES
Everything You Ever Wanted to Know About Everything: 10 Steps to Consciousness
Great Golf (with Dr. John Goode)
I Love Exercise
Kundalini Rising: The Ancient Egyptian Initiation Rite
Lose Weight
Magnetic Mind Toning: Relax, Listen and Master Your Mind
Meet Your Angel
Mer-Ka-Ba: Ascension to the 4th Dimension
Mommy Bunny's Going To Work
No More Alcohol
No More Sugar Junkie
Peace and Calm
Quit Smoking
Serenity Resonance Sound: Alpha/Theta Brain Waves (tape or CD)
Sex and Other Touchy Subjects (17 songs)
Sleep Beautiful Sleep
The Money Tape (with Joan Lessin)
The Violet Flame: The Most Beautiful Meditation in the World
Time Travel: 2 Past Life Journeys
Wellness Tape (with Dr. Lilia Prado, DO)
Yes I Can!: Motivate Yourself
Yoga Nidra/Hypnoyoga: The Ancient Oriental Method for Advancing Consciousness

VIDEO TAPES
Hypnotically Yours: Stockwell Interviews McGill, America's Most Beloved Hypnotist
McGill's Secrets of Magic & Stage Hypnosis: The Guardian Angel Show & How It's Done
Stockwell's Secrets of the Mind: Explore your Mind's Mystery and Mastery
Stockwell's Weight Loss Video
The Secret Lives of Ormond McGill: Stockwell Takes McGill on a Past Life Journey
Transformations: Demonstrations in Hypnosis/Channeling/Past Lives

To order books, audios, CD's and videotapes, see the back of this book.

THE SEARCH FOR COSMIC CONSCIOUSNESS

The Hypnosis Book Einstein Would Have Loved

BY **ORMOND McGILL, PH.D.**
AND **SHELLEY STOCKWELL, PH.D.**

CREATIVITY UNLIMITED PRESS ®
CREATIVITY UNLIMITED ®
30819 Casilina Drive
Rancho Palos Verdes, CA 90275
(310) 541-4844
E-Mail: sstockwell@earthlink.net
Web: www.shelleystockwell.com

ISBN 0912559-52-7
Library of Congress Catalog Card Number 99 098123
Printed in the United States of America

Photo of Einstein used with permission from Corbis/Bettman Images.

About Author Ormond McGill, Ph.D.

Ormond McGill, Ph.D. began his hypnosis career when he was 15 years old. At age 86, he is the celebrated Dean of American Hypnosis and Magic. He's traveled around the globe to exchange wisdom and secret and sacred teachings with other great shaman leaders.

A practicing hypnotherapist, stage hypnotist, hypnosis instructor and magician, Ormond has authored so many books, he's lost count. His newest book is *The Complete Encyclopedia of Hypnotherapy: The 21st Century Bible of Hypnotism*. He has appeared on numerous television programs from Art Linkletter in the 50's to recent appearances on The Learning Channel and the BBC.

Illustration by Shelley Stockwell

About Author Shelley Stockwell, Ph.D.

For over 21 years, author Shelley Stockwell, Ph.D. has been a practicing Transpersonal Hypnotherapist, Hypnosis Instructor, Motivational Speaker, Past Life Therapist, Trance Channel, Spiritual Counselor, Artist, Poet and Non-Denominational Minister. She holds her Ph.D. in Psychology.

Shelley trains and certifies thousands of students at her Creativity Learning Institute in Rancho Palos Verdes, California and on her enlightenment journeys to Egypt; Sedona, Arizona; and Bali, Indonesia. Her Certification Course in Spiritual Counseling is very popular.

Shelley is the Founder of the International Hypnosis Federation, an association that supports and promotes the good work of hypnotists, counselors, intuitives and healers. In 1999 she received the coveted Pen and Quill Award from the International Medical and Dental Hypnotherapy Association for outstanding writing in the field of hypnosis. Her television show: "The Shelley Show" won an Angel Award of Excellence for outstanding cable television. A popular guest on radio and television talk shows, she has appeared on The Phil Donohue Show, The Other Side, Mike and Maty, Strange Universe, Pajama Party, Good Morning Australia and multitudinous news programs. The National Enquirer calls her the "Hypnosis Expert."

She is the author of twelve books and dozens of audio and video tapes. Shelley lives with her family and cats in a house overlooking the Pacific Ocean. She collects turtles and likes to laugh.

You can contact her at the Creativity Learning Institute by calling (310) 541-4844 or you can e-mail her at sstockwell@earthlink.net. Visit Shelley's Website at shelleystockwell.com

ACKNOWLEDGEMENTS

Thanks to Susan Wagner, Steve Lamb and Wendy Munro for their proof reading, and to Nica Lee for her endless editing. Wendy Quintanilla for the fine cover of this book and all her help. I couldn't do it without you. Jon Nicholas for his tireless devotion and research. To our friends and students for their loving support. And, of course, we thank the primordial force that graced we mortals with Albert Einstein.

Cover Design and Book Format: Wendy Quintanilla
Editor: Nica Lee
Illustrations: Shelley Stockwell
Photos: Jon Nicholas and Bryce Stockwell

DEDICATION

**DEDICATED TO THE GENIUS OF
ALBERT EINSTEIN** who writes:

"The most beautiful and profound thing we can experience is the MYSTERIOUS. It is the source of all true art and science. He to whom emotion is a stranger, who can no longer wonder and stand rapt in awe, is as good as dead: his eyes are closed."

-Albert Einstein

PREFACE

"I like to think that the moon is there even if I'm not looking at it."
—Albert Einstein

Has this happened to you?

You are behaving yourself in the midst of a busy day when suddenly you stop short. A thrilling chill passes up your spine and you find yourself looking about with a new sense of perception. What seemed much like a muddy mess in a confusing and unclear world, suddenly sharpens into focus and becomes clear like crystal. You look up into the endless sky and your mind soars out into space. It seems that not only the Earth, but the entire Cosmos opens up to you and everything seems so simple. Everything is shipshape.

Then, as suddenly as it came, the thrilling chill is gone and you fall back into the muddy mess, feeling dopey as ever. Well, not quite. Somehow that flash of "knowing" puts warmth inside you that makes you feel at home.

Cosmic Consciousness is also called "Enlightenment" or "Illumination" for it comes unto you like a bright light while groping about in a dark room. Somehow, some way, everything shows up clearly. If the sudden turning on of the light causes you to bat your eyes a bit, enjoy the surprise! It's like opening a gift at Christmas.

What makes Cosmic Consciousness seem complex, is that you are searching for that which is already there. If you search in all the dark corners outside yourself, you'll never find it. If you want to find Cosmic Consciousness, light up and take a look within yourself.

THE SEARCH FOR COSMIC CONSCIOUSNESS is for you. It shows you how to light up; how to use your brain as a time-space machine.

We are at the start of a new century: 2000 AD. Some call it the Millennium. What is the millennium? Webster in his dictionary says it is a "period of great happiness and human perfection." That's a nice way of looking at it. The millennium is a wonder filled time to flick on the switch of your Cosmic Consciousness.

How do you do that?

That is your search!

Enlightenment can happen to anyone willing to explore their inner potential. The Transpersonal Hypnosis techniques in this book will help you understand and tame your mind.

Let's get going on your search for Cosmic Consciousness. You've quite a journey ahead of you. And, the nice part is, you don't even have to leave your seat to arrive at your destination. Have a great trip!

Shelley Stockwell, Ph.D. and Ormond McGill, Ph.D.
Rancho Palos Verdes, California, USA, 2000 AD

INTRODUCTION

"Cosmic Consciousness is a complex subject. If you wish to discover it, you will have to search."

−Albert Einstein

This book is based upon powerful scientific concepts and everyday conversations. It offers you stunning strategies to embrace consciousness and master your thoughts so you can be a mastermind. The 21st Century is a technological age. Computers are everywhere. You are intimately familiar with computers because you have one inside your head. It is a better time-space machine than any computer science has produced.

Where and what is your brain?

Where and what is your mind?

Where and what is consciousness?

Your brain/mind/consciousness is a dynamic, expanding, quantum universe evolving and born anew with each breath you take. Here you talk to yourself where YOU really live. Here you are one with space, time, matter, energy and GOD. Your bio-chemical brain wiring is different and distinct from anyone else's brain wiring. You are not the same person you were a moment before. And, not the same consciousness you were a moment ago. The entire universe is always in perpetual change and you are a miniature of the universe.

Ancient Egyptians mapped stars that they thought were close enough to touch. Ancient Greeks calculated earth's circumference and the distance to the moon. By 1100 AD, Chinese scholars had invented the seismograph, a magnetic compass and the idea that we have infinite empty space.

In 1915, Einstein's General Theory of Relativity showed that matter and energy, all the stuff in the universe, actually molds the flow of time and the shape of space. The "force" of gravity he said, is actually you and me following the shortest path through curved, four-dimensional space-time.

Today, we enter the millennium of mind. Our computer age with the computer's ability to crunch numbers lets us explore the smallest human cell and the biggest universe. The old alchemists were right when they said: "As above so below."

Electro-microscopes can now see things we've never seen before (yet they've always been there). We see things that are only a millionth of an inch in diameter. What we call "empty space," billions of light years away, is actually seething with activity on the subatomic levels as particles pop in and out of nothingness, say scientists.

The universe, your body and all matter once thought to be nothingness with no mass at all, is made up of neutrinos that weigh about one ten-millionth of the mass of an electron. Is there an even smaller unseen vast void? We are only now beginning to map this crucible of creation: THE VOID, The GodHead. What will your bio computer discover about this creative center of your very existence?

It took us over 100 million years to culturally catapult into a world of airplanes, computers, cyberspace and the awareness of vast universes of galaxies and voids. Now you will take your own quantum leap into the wormhole of your inner universe of limitless possibilities for harmony, balance and bliss. It is really quite simple.

THE SEARCH FOR COSMIC CONSCIOUSNESS

The Hypnosis Book Einstein Would Have Loved

YOUR STEP BY STEP GUIDE TO HIGHER CONSCIOUSNESS

- ★ Guidelines for Achieving a Peaceful Mind
- ★ Awaken the Kundalini
- ★ Telepathy, Thought Transference and Direct Perception
- ★ Boot Up Your Super Brain Computer
- ★ Become a Master Mind
- ★ Enjoy Self-Hypnosis
- ★ Secret and Sacred Meditations
- ★ Harness Your Dreams and Be Ecstatic
- ★ Discover and Develop Your Potential

Throughout all history, humans have searched for treasure: in sunken ships, in ancient tombs, in buried pirate loot, in lost gold mines, in stock market killings, in lottery winnings. Search... Search...Searching everywhere in places outside themselves, while little realizing that their greatest treasure is to be found buried within themselves. This book is a map to help you transform and find that treasure!

"The Cosmos looks like a great thought."

-Albert Einstein

The
Search

TABLE OF CONTENTS

PART ONE
WHAT IS COSMIC CONSCIOUSNESS?

Historical Mind Mapping
—by Shelley Stockwell

Plato: "Mind lives in the spherical head."
Mind your head, is what he said.

Aristotle: "Of course your mind is in the heart;
The warmest and most vital part."

"Forget the head. Forget the heart."
Said 17th century Frenchman **Descartes:**
"From these opinions I take issue.
Mind is separate from physical tissue.
Cogito, ergo sum;
Without a thought your life is done
If *I think therefore I am* is true;
You only exist if I think of you."

Photo by Jon Nicholas

"To see the world in a grain of sand, and heaven in a wildflower, hold infinity in the palm of your hand and eternity in an hour."

-William Blake

Chapter One
A PEEK AT CONSCIOUSNESS

The entire Universe is conscious. Everything that IS, is conscious to the degree of what IS. Bet you will run into this idea several times as you go through this book.

Cosmic Consciousness requires you to be conscious of consciousness. That's why, when a flash of satori or understanding comes in, suddenly it seems that now you know everything and you sense overwhelming bliss and oneness with all things.

Even if it takes eons of time, consciousness is forever evolving. Eons of time mean nothing to eternity, for in eternity, there is no time. Consciousness moves in quantum leaps of increasing awareness.

The Absolute Law of Cause and Effect
"The trouble with the world is that the stupid are cocksure and the intelligent are full of doubt."

-Bertrand Russell

In the past, physical science based its premise in the absolute law of Cause and Effect. This assertion made physical science finite. As nuclear physicists entered the world beyond cause and effect, uncertainty arose. Uncertainty gave science a new opportunity to think about existence and the infinite. Scientists chose to think beyond the limits of cause and effect. The more freedom to choose, the higher the level of consciousness. It was, the genius of Einstein. Always keep your mind open and questioning.

James Van Praag tells how a drop of his blood outside his body viewed under a microscope on a TV screen jumps around hysterically when he is told he must give up chicken. And then moves in a fluid gentle dance when he thinks of love.

Consciousness is an awareness of what IS. On this Earth walk, at this time, we know it mostly in four levels, with the possibility of a fifth. Your search for that fifth level is what this book is about.

THE FIVE LEVELS OF CONSCIOUSNESS
Level One: UNCONSCIOUS CONSCIOUSNESS ROCKS

"Few are those who see with their own eyes and feel with their own hearts."

-Albert Einstein

Unconscious consciousness is the degree of consciousness we find in a rock, a stone or any inorganic matter. A rock is not aware like a human. In the realm of unconscious consciousness, freedom does not exist. It is "sushupt," as they say in the East. Sushupt is Sanskrit for "absolute sleep." Sleep, in which not even dreams stir. Matter is not dead. It is waiting for its consciousness to grow. It is like a seed.

Sphere
The earth is worth her girth in mirth.
The merry land where we lie and stand.
She embraces us in gravity
Regardless of color or depravity.
Glues us on water, snow and ground,
Regularly makes us come around.
She runs hot and cold, is third from the sun,
And weighs in at 6.6 sextillion short tons!
For her global support and latitude
(Forgive me for the platitude)
I offer Earth my gratitude.

-Shelley Stockwell

Level Two: PLANT CONSCIOUSNESS
This is the degree of consciousness we find in plants, trees and flowers. A plant is certainly more conscious than a rock, but it still has slight self-consciousness. The vegetation kingdom is conscious of its environment. Plants respond to music, loving words and tender care.

They protect themselves and warn others of perceived danger. Plants generate an array of chemicals that protect them against disease and help them to reproduce. But, vegetation does not have the same fullness of perception of self as other levels of consciousness.

Level Three: ANIMAL CONSCIOUSNESS

In the animal kingdom, we find the beginning of self consciousness. It is not fully developed but is obviously there. The animal is aware of itself. Animals are aware of the collective group to which they belong. Most animals are aware of instinctive feelings and past experiences: e.g., when hungry, an animal knows it's time to eat. When tired, an animal knows it is time to rest. When an animal feels sexual, it knows it's time to mate. Some animals even plan for the future. Most animals main focus is reacting to the here and now and protecting continuing life. Animals have limited self consciousness. Animals may achieve cosmic consciousness but because of our language barriers, we don't know for sure at this time.

Level Four: SELF CONSCIOUSNESS

We humans, like animals, are instinctive and react with basic urges and impulses. Plus, we recognize self. Humans have a glimmering that there is something special about themselves related to Cosmic Consciousness.

Some human beings are unaware of Cosmic Consciousness.

Some are aware of Cosmic Consciousness but do little about it.

Some occasionally seek Cosmic Consciousness but never fully achieve it.

Some diligently seek Cosmic Consciousness but never fully achieve it.

And a few who seek, achieve Cosmic Consciousness.

In your regular perception of consciousness, you are Homo Sapien. When you expand to Cosmic Consciousness, you evolve into Homo Superior. Why not? Your potential is astronomical.

Level Five: COSMIC CONSCIOUSNESS

"Only one who devotes himself to a cause with his whole strength and soul can be a true master. For this reason mastery demands all of a person."

-Albert Einstein

Cosmic Consciousness is the paramount form of consciousness. You are both small and vast. YOU ARE A MINIATURE OF THE UNIVERSE AND THE UNIVERSE IS A VAST MACROCOSM OF YOU. There is no difference between you and the Whole of Existence. Relativity answers that question. Albert told you so!

Cosmic Consciousness is like a BRIGHT LIGHT that reveals TRUTH. With it you KNOW the universal and eternal nature of your true Self. With this knowing, your entire being is infused with DIVINE LOVE; which is your true nature. Cosmic Consciousness is an experiential realization, from deep inside of you. With Cosmic Consciousness, you come to know that the immortal BEING that you are, is directly linked with the TOTALITY. You see yourself as standing in the very center of the entire universe.

What will the experience of Cosmic Consciousness be like for you?

This is highly individual. You, as an individual consciousness, are unique in all EXISTENCE. Some say the experience is like a bursting bombshell as everything appears to be illuminated with bright light and/or sparkling colors.

Others say it comes in like a delightful swimming sensation, as though you had been set afloat in a warm pool of utter contentment.

Some say that what seemed too complicated to understand suddenly is easy to understand. In other words, the complex becomes simple.

Others say they seem to know all about what IS and are immediately harmonious with the universal scheme of things.

All report Cosmic Consciousness as being a wonderful experience.

How will you know when you experience Cosmic Consciousness? Guess you'll have to experience it and then you'll know.

Enlightenment and the Kundalini

To enlighten means to give spiritual insight. "The Enlightenment" was an 18th century philosophical movement that emphasized universal human progress and the use of reason. As you alter normal consciousness, your journey may move you into the amazing realm of transcendental states of awareness.

The Kundalini is a form of energy associated with the feeling of being alive—filled with freely moving energy—flooded with light, or enlightenment. This is a first-hand experience of the body opening through the central nervous system via the spine and the seven chakras:

1st Chakra: The base of your spine
2nd Chakra: Sexual organs
3rd Chakra: Solar plexus
4th Chakra: Heart
5th Chakra: Throat
6th Chakra: Third eye (in the middle of your forehead)
7th Chakra: Top of your head

The Kundalini releases emotional or karmic "blocks." As the chakras clear and open, releasing freely moving energy, you are flooded with a myriad of physical and emotional experiences. Experiencing the Kundalini is an on-going process, lasting from several months to many years. As the energy moves through your body, it clears away blocking impurities or imbalances. It leaves you with an experience of being fully alive, reborn, and reawakened into a full feeling (fulfilling) experience of resonating energy. Joseph Campbell called it: "Feeling the rapture of being alive."

7000 years ago Yogis used the Sanskrit word "Kundalini." They believed that without its energy, no enlightenment was possible. "The Kundalini," they said, "is the central energy of all life." At death, this "energy cocoon" leaves the body and determines the nature of each reincarnation. The patterns of movement, as energy travels through the body, varies slightly from culture to culture. Yet every pattern corresponds to the central nervous system. All agree that as the different centers are activated, a person's spiritual awakening intensifies.

Many experience the Kundalini spontaneously, as a result of a key event, such as a near-death experience or childbirth. Spontaneous Kundalini awakening can also be stimulated by hypnosis, acupuncture, energy-balancing, meditation, Rolfing and touch therapies. Learning to contact and express the truth stimulates the Kundalini.

The process of enlightenment can be quite dramatic. In fact, those who do not understand, might inaccurately label a person who is having a spiritual emergency, as psychotic. This puts a Kundalini soul in a peculiar dilemma. Their "spirit body" is being profoundly lifted into the sacred hand of God, while their physical self might be chastised, exorcised or even committed!

Spiritual opening often happens spontaneously during hypnotherapy and counseling. So, it is critical that every counselor and therapist be aware of the tell-tale signs of a Kundalini awakening and honor it. You will be renewed and truly transformed. Fortunately, today there is a renaissance of truth and introspection, as we collectively embark on the Kundalini journey of an awakened world.

SIGNPOSTS OF THE KUNDALINI

The following objective or subjective signposts mark purification and balancing. The results will be greater emotional stability, enhanced intuition, and a feeling of peace.

BODY SENSATIONS
Deep ecstatic tingling vibration.
Feelings of orgasm.
Feeling hot and cold.
Actually seeing light internally.
Visions of inner light.
The "Aha!" experience.

HEARING SOUNDS
Strong sounds and voices heard from the inside.

FEELING DISCOMFORT
Headaches or focused sensations in any region of your body that begin and end abruptly.

TIME DISTORTION
Thoughts speed up, slow down, or stop. Spontaneous trance states.

VISUAL BALANCING
Simultaneously seeing the inner and outer.

DETACHMENT
A sense of watching yourself.

OUT OF BODY EXPERIENCE
Feeling that you are away from your physical body.

INTENSE EMOTIONS
Ecstasy, bliss, cosmic harmony.
Occasionally fear, anger, depression, or confusion followed by peace, love and contentment.

INCREASED ESP
Increased intuitive powers and ability to see auras.
Natural psychics are more likely to have a Kundalini awakening.

TEMPORARY PARALYSIS
Involuntary positioning of body, limbs, or fingers.

WHY NOT TAKE A GUIDE?

"When a blind beetle crawls over the surface of the globe, he doesn't realize that the track he has covered is curved. I was lucky enough to have spotted it."

-Albert Einstein

Some say that you can advance more quickly if you take a guide with you to help. Guides make the journey fun. What Master guide will YOU take? Choose a Master with a similar nature to your own.

You can call your guide: God, Yahweh or Great Mystery

If you are sentimental: Christ, Mary, or Diana.

If you are intellectual: Buddha.

If you are playful: try Shiva.

If you are scientific: Patanjali or Saraswati is appreciated.

If you enjoy every moment of your life: Krishna may capture your heart.

If you are serene and peaceful, there is none greater than Lao Tzu or Quan Yin.

Or, you can discover another special guide within yourself right this instant. There are many great masters. When you are ready, the appropriate master appears.

Which Master is best? There is no greater or best. All masters tell the same truth in their own way. So make your selection and choose the ONE you'd most like for a companion in your SEARCH FOR COSMIC CONSCIOUSNESS. The Universe is perfectly willing to meet you on your own terms.

HYPNOTIC HELPER:

Shelley Stockwell's audiotape, *Meet Your Angel: The Closed Eye Meditation of Love and Light,* helps you discover your personal guidance. You can order it using the order form in the back of this book.

*"Relativity teaches us the connection
between the different descriptions
of one and the same reality."*

–Albert Einstein

Chapter Two

THE TRINITY THAT IS YOU

Y ou are a trinity of Body and Mind and Consciousness. The more you learn about the triple nature of yourself, the more rapidly you can complete your search for Cosmic Consciousness. Let's explore what that really means:

YOUR BODY

Your body is the outer physical self that you see in the mirror. It moves you, nourishes you and pleasures you. When imbalanced, it may even pain you. Your body is used to manifesting your behavior in the physical world of three-dimensional space. This remarkable mechanism in which you dwell, is not immortal. When it dies, you will leave this dwelling. But, you'll still be alive as an individual consciousness. Within your head is your brain, which functions as your behavioral bio-computer.

YOUR MIND

Your mind is intangible. You can't put your finger on it. It is the process that your SELF uses to operate your physical body. You can use it effectively or ineffectively. It can elevate you to a genius or drop you into insanity. The more effectively you use your mind, the more you advance your consciousness. Your mind lets you pick up this book and is reading these words. You are making meaning of these words via your miraculous biochemical and electromagnetic mind. Your mind produces thoughts, which manifest through and within your body on three levels: Conscious, Subconscious and Superconscious. The more you understand how to use these levels, the more you increase your awareness or consciousness. Let's explore your conscious, subconscious and superconscious levels each in turn:

Level 1. Conscious Phase of Mind

The conscious mind is the mask you use to interface with the world. The word personality comes from the Latin word *persona* and means *coming through a mask*. Your conscious mind controls your personality and the stories you tell yourself and others. It keeps you physically aware.

You use your conscious mind to shift attention from one thing to another. It is your logical and analytical mode. It protects your body from danger by critically judging, evaluating and weighing information, one idea at a time. It makes decisions based upon information it lets in or deletes. In other words, your conscious mind focuses upon the thoughts you think. As you think…so you become.

Level 2. Subconscious Phase of Mind

Your subconscious is the home of your individual personality, emotions, feelings and instinctive behaviors. It drives to survive and gives you your human potential. A pattern-making and pattern-repeating device, your subconscious mind self-conducts the majority of your brain functions.

Your subconscious is the inner operation of mind that keeps your body going. It controls your automatic, biochemical responses: your heart beating, your lungs operating and every muscle, nerve, ligament and organ working. Your subconscious mind fights disease and returns you to homeostasis. It's doing an excellent job of keeping you active, balanced and alive, or you wouldn't be reading this right now.

Where are thoughts when you're not thinking them?

The subconscious mind! It has perfect memory. The archive of your subconscious remembers all information about you, and from these memories draws conclusions. Your subconscious mind stubbornly causes you to be who and what it believes you are. If you want to listen to the voice of your subconscious, listen to your thoughts and babble while you are alone or talking to others. The words you use create your reality and your life. Hypnosis influences the subconscious mind.

Illustration by Shelley Stockwell

Sublime

Level 3. Superconscious Phase of Mind

The superconscious mind is your BIG picture. It encompasses and permeates *all* levels of consciousness with its expanded awareness and perception. It oversees the conscious and subconscious phases of mind, and remembers your experiences within and beyond your current lifetime. This realm of transcendental joy bypasses the time-space continuum so you easily explore past, future and between-life memory.

Your superconscious awareness knows your truth, dreams and the steps you need to take to make your life work perfectly. All personal transformation, healing and bliss tap this consciousness.

Your superconscious mind, when freed, knows your destiny and life purpose. Your higher self blesses you with profound wisdom. Here, you discover and connect with your life force energy and all living things. Here, you enjoy your intuitive spiritual gifts, have peak experiences and commune with God in your own personal way. Sometimes called the Collective Unconscious, the Akashic Records, the Great Book or The Book of Remembrance, your super conscious mind is your own private genie in a bottle.

Your superconscious mind is your connection with the cosmos. It is the phase of mind you use when you achieve Cosmic Consciousness.

The Stockwell Mind Map

CONSCIOUS	SUBCONSCIOUS	SUPER CONSCIOUS
Outer Self Physical Awareness	**Inner Self** Internal Awareness	**Higher Self** Expanded Awareness
Left brain	Right brain	All brain
Stories we tell ourselves.	Attitudes, beliefs, habits.	Inspiration, creative imagination.
Concrete Analytical Logical, critical, protective, defensive.	**Emotional** Literal Bio-chemical, autonomic response, body function, survival instinct.	**Ephemeral** Airy-fairy Aura/unconditional love.
Co-creates with the subconscious and super conscious.	Co-creates with the conscious and super conscious.	Brings inner and outer harmony and balance to all parts of self.
Some short term memory.	Most memory: uncritically accepts, records and stores data from the outside world. Combines stored data into hunches and answers, language.	Remembers connection to all, universal wisdom, life purpose, spiritual guidance, God, inner knower, silent witness, light.
Honors linear time, aware of now analyzes past might project future.	Honors non-linear time, aware of past.	Transcends linear time and space knows all and "future" simultaneous reception.
Personality	Most Sub-personalities	Beyond personality. Metaphors, archetypes, symbols.
Keyboard	Software	Hard drive
Practical	Emotional	Soulful
Waking states	Hypnotic states	Lucid dreams
Body	Mind	Spirit
Son	Father	Holy ghost
Ego	Id	Super Ego
Earth	Sky	Cosmos
Play a record	Record a record	Invent a record
Eros	Shadow	Spirit
Basic self-child	Conscious self-adult	Higher self-parent
Caterpillar	Cocoon	Butterfly

YOUR CONSCIOUSNESS

Your consciousness is your immortal SELF. The more you become aware of consciousness, the more you advance toward Cosmic Consciousness. Your consciousness is also called spirit. It uses your mind to speak to you. Consciousness/Spirit is the elemental immortal YOU. It is the individual "I AM," the only one exactly like you in the entirety of Existence. Becoming conscious of your immortal consciousness IS Cosmic Consciousness.

"The important thing is to keep questioning.
Curiosity has its own reason for existing. One cannot help
but be in awe when contemplating the mysteries of eternity,
of life, of the marvelous structure of reality. It is enough if one
tries merely to comprehend a little of this mystery every day.
Never lose a holy curiosity."

-Albert Einstein

Chapter Three
YOUR SUPER BRAIN-COMPUTER

Through mind, you will come to know consciousness. But how are you going to find mind? Mind is elusive. It is like the path a bird leaves behind as it flies through the sky. Stop chasing these bird paths, and just say mind is a process for producing thoughts, and that mind is the programmer of your Super Brain-Computer.

Inside your head is a super-duper computer. A bio-computer far greater in potential than any electronic computer yet manufactured. It has billions and billions of connectors. Let's take a look at how your Super Brain-Computer is constructed and operates.

Stem Cells

Your brain/mind and all the tissue that makes up your physical psychodynamic structure began after you, the egg, chose you, the sperm, to fertilize itself.

You began as a "blastocyte" or hollow blob like sphere of 15 or 20 stem cells. For the briefest time (a day or two) everything was possible for you as these translucent dots of life. You had the capacity to become any tissue you needed. Skin. Hair. Nerve. Bone. Blood vessel. The lens of an eye. You grew yourself into 210 other known cell types transforming one cell into a clump and finally a complex of tissue. You shape shifted yourself into any and every tissue and organ in your body.

Slightly more specialized, stem cells developed in your brain and nervous system. They give you the ability to repair and restore your own brain!

Most interesting of all is that: *Stem cells, kept in the right environment, are immortal.* **You are immortal.**

Your Brain-Computer

Your brain inside your head, is divided into four regions: forebrain, endbrain, midbrain and hindbrain. It is also speculated that you have a "brain" buried in the midsection of your body. Each region performs specific mental activity, as directed by your mind. Through the brain, you observe, think, and do as you consciously relate to the world. These functions are called "Critical Mind" or "Conscious Mind." Actually, this is a misnomer, as there is no tangible mind in the brain. Mind is immortal. Brain is not immortal. When the body turns to dust, so does the brain.

The right lobe of your brain is generally designed for handling creative and intuitive thoughts. While the left lobe deals mostly with analytical and practical work. The base portion of brain, an enlarged continuation of your spine, is critical to life in the body. It deals with your instinctive responses. Emerging from the interior of the base brain are twelve cranial nerves. From the base of the skull, they are distributed to various parts of the head and neck where they direct the functioning of special senses and bodily operations. Death by hanging is said to be caused by pressure on this base brain or medulla, not by strangulation.

Buried in your solar plexus, you'll discover your *abdominal brain*. The word "solar" in solar plexus, like a sun, is the center of your body. It provides you with energy via its filaments that extend like the rays of sun into your abdominal organs. In Japan, this brain is called *the Hara*, or *Seat of the Soul*. In India, it is regarded as the *Center of Being* and the great reservoir of your life force or *Prana*. Your abdominal brain operates via the autonomic sympathetic and parasympathetic nervous system. The parasympathetic nervous system regulates and energizes your body's inner functions that your life depends upon.

While each portion of the brain is designed to specialize in specific functions, all portions naturally interact together in producing your SUPER BRAIN-COMPUTER. It functions as a bio-physical space-time transducer. The ancient Chinese said: "The Tao (universe) is in your head." Your Super Brain-Computer's potentials are astronomical. You may have scarcely learned how to operate your computer's keyboard or command keys, let alone your amazing computer brain. When you do…WOW! What amazing things appear upon the screen!

Just like your handy computer sitting upon your desk, your brain computer needs someone to program and operate it. That "someone" is your mind. Cosmic Consciousness employs your mind to program your super brain-computer to produce the thoughts you desire. Thoughts are "forms" of energy through which you make your body perform, as you elect it to perform. Thought-forms determine the way you perform, and the way you live in the world.

The more you learn, the more elaborate the neural networks and the more your brain weights. Helper, or oligodendroglia cells speed communication among brain or neural cells.

Albert Einstein's brain had four times more oliGODendroglia cells than any other gifted brains studied at UCLA. When he died of a ruptured abdominal aorta at age 76, his brain was removed and preserved. Two areas on the side of his brain, called the inferior parietal regions, were 15% wider than other brains studied. This "swelling" diverted a brain groove called The Sylvan Fissure, and made space for an expanse of integrated cortical networks.

Function effects structure and structure effects function.

Photo by Jon Nicholas

"My religion consists of a humble admiration of the illimitable superior spirit who reveals himself in the slight details we are able to perceive with our frail and feeble mind."

-Albert Einstein

Chapter Four
THE ABDOMINAL BRAIN

Where do you think your Subconscious Mind lives in your body? The subconscious mind is the cornerstone of the hypnotherapy profession. Psychologists and hypnotherapists have long speculated as to where in your brain you'll find your so-called "Subconscious Mind."

Early in the 20th Century, William Walker Atkinson advanced the interesting idea that the seat of the subconscious is found in THE SOLAR PLEXIS. Atkinson, a man miles ahead of his time said: *"The Solar Plexus is the brain's center of feeling."* Have you noticed that when emotions strike you strongly, you do not feel it in your head, you feel it in your gut?

Prove it to yourself...

You are speeding down the highway; a patrol car drives up with sirens; you stop. A policeman gets out. You experience a sinking sensation. Where? In your stomach.

You receive some good news and you feel happiness. Where? In your abdomen.

You hear some bad news and it causes a knot in the pit of your stomach.

Do you get butterflies in your stomach with stage fright or a love interest?

Such reactions are your subconscious abdominal brain in action. Your abdominal brain works with and stimulates the reasoning portions of your brain. Gut level response is a total brain response.

There is a direct relationship between emotional states and the physical body. Fear and suspense are not felt in the head but, in the pit of the stomach.

The Law of Body/Mind Reciprocity
"Mind affects the body and body affect the mind."

The heart beats rapidly when we are excited, angry or in love. Emotional states react upon the physical organs of the body, producing physiological changes in them. Emotions often influence the health or lack of health in the parts of the body affected.

The way your mental computer is programmed to operate has much to do with how you feel. *"Mind affects the body and body affects the mind."* For example:

Breathing stale air in a poorly ventilated room can make you mentally sluggish.

Your thoughts effect your sexual response.

Physical indigestion can cause mental depression.

Mental depression can make you feel physically rotten, super sensitive or feel nothing at all. Depression causes aches and pains, heart palpitations, difficult breathing, dizziness, headaches, digestive problems, constipation, diarrhea, arthritis-like symptoms, shingles and upper respiratory infections. In return, these maladies exacerbate depression. Depression can cause illness and illness can cause depression. Chronic illness, like gastric ulcers, irritable bowel syndrome, colitis, headaches, migraines, sinus problems, asthma, arthritis, fibromylgia and chronic fatigue syndrome, contribute to or activate depressing changes in brain chemistry.

"The first symptoms of poor blood circulation" says, Dr. H.A. Parkyn, "appear in your head." Poor memory, the inability to concentrate, sleeplessness, nervousness, headaches and then poor circulation result. The poorer the circulation the poorer the circulation until you are out of circulation entirely.

The Law of Emotional Reciprocity
"No emotion is completely experienced until its physical response is expressed."

It is a "law" of body/mind cooperation that: *"No emotion is completely experienced until its physical response is expressed."* Let's say the emotion of anger arises. It will not be completed until it is expressed as a biochemical response in some part of your body; i.e., a scowl on your forehead, compression of your lips, muscular tension of your hands and/or quickening of your heart. You don't feel angry until you *feel angry*.

All physical responses commence with an idea in mind, a reaction in the body and then reflect back upon the mind. It is a circling between mind and body; body and mind. Modern terminology calls it a biofeedback operation or cybernetic feedback response.

Mental and emotional expression does not come to fruition until expressed in a physical response in the abdominal brain. Understanding this is vital to the effective use of hypnosis.

To paraphrase the famous psychologist, William James: *"Bodily changes directly follow the perception of feelings and emotions. Particular perceptions produce widespread bodily effects of immediate physical influence, antecedent to the arousal of an emotion or emotional idea. Every bodily change is felt acutely or obscurely, the moment it occurs. If we fancy some strong emotion and then try to subtract from our consciousness the feelings of its bodily symptoms, we have nothing left behind. A disembodied human emotion is a sheer nonentity. For us, emotion dissociated from all bodily feelings is inconceivable. Feelings are constituted by and made up of the physical changes we call our 'expressions of emotion.' In order to control subconscious behavior, (i.e., regulate and direct your emotional nature) all habits, phobias and neurotic responses must begin by regulating the activity of the abdominal brain."*

Do you say "yea" or "nay" to William's opinion? Either way say: "Thank you William?" He helps you come up with your own opinion.

Your cerebro-spinal nervous system is controlled by the cerebrum, the physical processor of thoughts and ideas, which is directly connected with the parasympathetic nervous system that is controlled by the solar plexus. The abdominal brain is the seat of feelings.

Your brain is hooked up with your mental computer by many delicate nerve filaments. These "connecting nerves" both send and receive (efferent and afferent). Like telegraph wires connecting two great systems, these nerves pass the messages that cause your physical state to influence your mental state, and your mental state to arouse your physical state.

If you are upset, physical and emotional responses disturbs your liver, stomach, bowels, spleen, glands, sinuses and corresponding disturbances in the mind. Ideas held in the mind arouse activity and sensations of physical organs, muscles, nerves and ligaments. If the ideas are positive, their effect is beneficial. If the ideas are negative, their effect is harmful. Without such linkage between the physical and emotional systems, life in the body would be impossible.

Your brain is always with you. Talk and discuss with it; like you would with a best friend. Many people mutter trivia. But, you can talk with your brain about serious things; actual problems you wish help in solving. Together you can work things out. You can talk to your brain about delightful things; ways to bring yourself joy and expanded wisdom.

Who is talking with the brain? Your SELF (your consciousness) is talking. If dealing with an intellectual problem, talk to the left lobe. If an artistic or inventive consideration, talk to the right lobe. If it has something to do with your emotions or body function, talk to your solar plexus. You might even give the different portions of your brain nicknames. Say: "Professor" for the left lobe, "Inventor" for the right lobe and "Doc" for your solar plexus.

Speak right out loud when you discuss things with the various portions of your brain. But, better do this in private, for if people outside hear you doing this, they will very likely think you're nuts.

When you get good advice from your Super Brain-Computer, say "THANK YOU!" You have just received another gift. Whatever comes along in your life, be it good, bad, pleasant or unpleasant, be thankful you can experience it. Experiencing is proof that you are. That YOU ARE, is miraculous.

"We are like a little child entering a huge library.
The walls are covered to the ceiling with books in many
different tongues. The child knows that someone must
have written these books. It does not know who or how.
It does not understand the languages in which they
are written. But the child notes a definite plan in the
arrangement of the books…a mysterious order which
it does not comprehend, but only dimly suspects."

-Albert Einstein

Chapter Five

ENERGIZING YOUR MIND

Your mind and brain work closely together. Mind programs your brain-computer, which controls the way your body functions in this immediate space and time. When you energize your mind, you simultaneously turn up your brainpower and empower your body. In reverse, as you bring energy into your body, you increase your mental energy. Mind/Body is a circling of energies.

Mind is a process for producing thoughts. Mind functions as the programmer of your brain-computer. Thoughts are things. Thoughts are forms of energy arranged in patterns called thought forms. The more effectively you learn to use your mind, the more powerful the thought forms you produce. Powerful thought forms influence outside of you, and across space.

The mind programming the brain-computer is like an electrical step-down transformer. It steps up the current, and the nervous system provides the wiring that conveys current throughout the body to make the body perform. Mind produces thoughts that the brain amplifies. The stronger the amplification, the more powerfully thoughts influence the inside and outside of the body, via THOUGHT TRANSFERENCE. Thought transference is a power you can use to advance consciousness. Some call this powerful transmission of thought from one person to another; thought projection.

Thought Projection

Have you ever been with someone and it's like you can read each others mind?

Thought projection is like energy passed between two coils of wire spaced apart. One coil is electrically stimulated with an alternating current and its power is transmitted through space, via electromagnetic energy to the second coil. The second coil responds to the same frequency or period of change as the first coil.

In the Orient, this concept is more romantic. Mind is likened to a lake of still water. If I transfer a thought to you, my thought causes ripples to occur on my lake and you obtain similar ripples on your lake.

Thought transference energy appears to be of two types: *magnetic energy* or *raw energy* that is generated within the body, and *telepathic energy* that transmits the raw energy inside and outward into the world. The two work together as a unit. Together they energize "thought form" which, in turn, further energize the mind. It is a biofeedback process.

Telepathic energy is the product of thought. Every thought produces electric-like discharges in the brain-computer and electric-like discharges produce a wave. A thought wave is much like a radio wave, only much subtler, and it can be transmitted through space. When this transmitted "thought form" is powered by the raw energy, the result is THOUGHT PROJECTION.

How Do You Generate Raw Energy Within Yourself?

Try this wonderful exercise. The energy of the universe is motion. To amass universal energy, do this. You will be amazed at the results.

Sit in a chair, extend your arms in front of yourself and start shaking your hands vigorously. Shake them in any direction, anyway they want to go. Just shake them wildly, in absolute freedom. You start with effort but soon the shaking will become effortless and it will seem to occur almost by itself. As you do this, allow your mind to grow calm and experience yourself as the shaking. The time will come when it seems that it is no longer your hands that are shaking, rather it is YOU who are shaking, both inside and outside.

When you become the shaking rather than just doing the shaking, you will feel yourself filling with energy; an energy that somehow seems both mental and physical, at the same time.

After you become the shaking, relax your hands in your lap and rest a bit.

You are now ready to shake your entire body. This brings in even greater vital energy.

Stand erect, close your eyes and allow your whole body to vibrate. You'll find this easy to do, as you have already started the energy flow. Allow your whole body to become energy. Allow your body to melt and dissolve its boundaries. Stand relaxed, loose and natural. You do not have to do anything; you are simply there waiting. All you have to do is cooperate and allow it to happen. Cooperation should be effortless. Just allow it to be. You will find your body starting to make movements on its own. What movements it makes depends on you; everyone is different. Possibly your head will twitch and your body will start shaking in different ways. Just allow it to take on the shaking freely and shake any way it wants to.

Your body may make subtle movements like a little dance. Your hands move, your legs move, seemingly on their own and your entire body will start shaking with subconscious movement all over. All you have to do is let the shaking happen.

This energy is very subtle, so do not resist it. Just allow it to develop on its own. As it does, think of the shaking as the energy of the universe coming into you. When you have had enough of this automatic shaking of your body, just stop. You can stop anytime you please.

Now, stand still with your eyes closed and breathe deeply and fully while directing this energy towards your brain. Visualize and imagine your brain as a glowing ball of energy passing through every nerve and permeating every fiber of your being. In your mind's eye, see, hear, feel, smell and taste the energy flowing throughout your entire body. You are alive with energy. Use your imagination in doing this. Never be afraid to use your imagination. Imagination is the creative power of the mind. Everything starts in the imagination.

Now, how do you feel? Do you feel yourself alive with vital energy? Test it for yourself:

Extend your arms and direct the energy into your hands and you will feel your fingers tingle as though an electrical current were passing out of them. Bring the fingertips of each hand towards the other, spaced about an inch apart. Experience the flow of energy between your hands. Touch your fingertips together in front of a black cloth; then separate them a little and move them back and forth an inch each way. Observe what is there. You will see lines of misty radiance flowing between them. You can see them because they are there!

You have just learned how to generate raw energy in yourself. This raw energy can be used to influence yourself (within your own body) and to influence others (outside of your own body). Place, on top of this raw energy, your thoughts (or telepathic energy) and you perform an oriental method of hypnosis.

How to Perform Mental Telepathy

Let's learn how to project thought with the raw energy that you have learned to generate.

Telepathic energy is easy to produce. Its production is an automatic function of your mind. Every thought produces telepathic energy. Telepathy can be strengthened by attention and will. *Attention* means to hold a thought consistent and centered in your mind. *Will* means to direct a thought where you want it to go and/or to create the effects you wish it to produce. You can project the energy to influence your mental process or direct it towards someone else. You do this by programming your brain-computer.

How can you be more effective in transmitting raw energy as thought forms?

Do it effortlessly. Do not concentrate hard on the thought or try to push it by an effort of will. Relax. Do it softly. If you are uptight and try too hard, you won't be able to transmit thought. Thought does not go through 3-dimensional space. Thought goes through hyperspace.

Thought goes through the 4th dimension. Thought is here and then it is there. WILL is not used to push thoughts. WILL is only used to form the thought and place it in the center of the mind where it is visualized.

Gently place a goal into the center of your mind. The center of your mind is called the septum lucidum (or pelucidum). Imagine that directly in from your third eye (between your eyebrows) and directly down from your crown (the center of the fontenal, or soft spot you had as a baby) you have a meeting point. That is the center of your mind. Your goal can be internal (within yourself) or external (in the physical world). Picture and imagine your goal in the center of your mind and relax. It will melt like a candle into your consciousness and become your reality.

If you want to project this goal or notion to another, gently release it through your third eye into their third eye.

Practice bringing up your energy, centering attention and directing your will with gentle thoughts. This allows telepathy to move. Practice it often.

THROUGH MIND...CONSCIOUSNESS IS KNOWN. MENTALLY PICTURE AND IMAGINE YOUR GOAL.

HYPNOTIC HELPER:

The Mer-Ka-Ba is an ancient Egyptian initiation rite that uses sacred geometry and breath to take you to the 4th dimension. It is available from the list at the back of this book.

PART TWO
BECOME A MASTERMIND

"*I sometimes ask myself how it came about that I was the one to develop the theory of relativity. The reason, I think, is that the normal adult never stops to think about problems of space and time. These are things, which he has thought about as a child. But my intellectual development was retarded. As a result, I began to wonder about space and time only when I had really grown up.*"

-Albert Einstein

Photo by Jon Nicholas

*"I have no particular talent.
I am merely inquisitive."*

-Albert Einstein

Chapter Six

CONTROLLING YOUR MIND

M ind may be intangible but its operation in producing thought is decidedly tangible. Thoughts your mind produces programs your Super Brain and determines your behavior.

To control your mind, begin by recognizing that you are not your mind. You use your mind but that mind is not YOU. You are your SELF, a consciousness that uses mind to think with and to produce thoughts. Here are the three basic rules for controlling your mind:

THE FIRST RULE: Make your mind think what you want it to think

Your mind has long had freedom to think whatever it wants to think; therefore it is easy to feel that it controls you. Reverse this process and recognize that your mind is only an activity you decide to engage in. Mind is used as you choose. Learn to regulate mind as though it were a mechanism you turn on and off at will. Learn to do this for yourself, and then you can help others do it. A mind out-of-control is the basis for mental disturbance.

THE SECOND RULE: Make your mind stop thinking when you do not want it to think

For many, mind has been allowed to bring in random thoughts and it may seem like your mind does your thinking for you. Random thoughts can be a confusing and disturbing shamble without organization. To correct this, master your mind instead of letting it master you. Use your mind when you want to use it, and do not use it when you do not want to use it. Most importantly, learn to make your mind become silent when you want it to be silent.

Look upon your mind as a mechanism you use to think with, and you make it think because you want it to think, not because it makes you think. This brings in the awareness that you can operate your mind precisely as you wish. Mastering your mind instead of your mind mastering you, transforms you into a Mastermind.

To be able to "turn off your mind" may seem a paradox, as the word mind conveys everything you think is important to your life. How then can you "turn it off" without losing your mind? "Turn off your mind" does not mean you lose your mind. You cannot exist without your mind. But you can learn to control it; to stop thinking when you want to become quiet. Mind is just an activity. Think of your mind like this:

You talk and you say you are talking. What is talking?

If you stop talking, where is the talking? Talking is nothing tangible, it is just an activity. Mind is precisely like that. Just as you can control the process of talking, you can also control the process of thinking.

When you become a Mastermind, you make your mind think what and when you want it to think and to stop thinking when you want it to stop thinking.

THE THIRD RULE: Become a witness to the thought you think

The more proficient you become at witnessing your thoughts (as though from a distance viewing), the more control you develop over your mind. Witness your thoughts in all forms of mental activity. Make witnessing thoughts your habitual way of thinking. In doing this, you greatly alter your perception and you'll soon recognize that it is your SELF doing the actual thinking, not your mind.

These rules apply to controlling your mind. Up to this point, the operation of your mind may have seemed pretty much hit-or-miss. Sometimes your thinking is reliable; sometimes unreliable. Your thinking has produced constructive thoughts and destructive thoughts. Discipline your mind and you can use it to always produce only constructive thoughts.

An Oriental proverb says that mind is like a jumpy monkey, the more you try to control the monkey, the more restless the monkey gets. The best way to control the monkey is to just leave it alone and allow it to control itself. Mind is like that; if you wish to control your mind, do not try to control it. Just let it be. Let your mind do whatever it is doing but do not allow yourself to become identified with the thinking it does. Become a witness to whatever your mind conjures, as though you were watching a motion picture upon the screen and don't be concerned with what your mind is picturing. BECOME A WITNESS TO YOUR THOUGHTS.

Do not think that because you had this thought that it is profound and has meaning. It is just a thought. Nothing more, nothing less. Be as unconcerned about what your mind is doing as if it didn't belong to you. Do that and you will soon get your mind under control. It will continue to produce thoughts because you have helped it produce thoughts. Cooperate with your mind, and it will be under control.

That is discipline.

This controlled method provides a remarkable form of self-hypnosis. As you take control of your subconscious mind, it becomes reconditioned in its habit of thinking. This will be discussed later in this book.

When your mind tells you the truth about yourself, always say: "*Thank you for sharing.*"

*"When I examine myself and my methods of thought,
I come to the conclusion that the gift of fantasy has meant more
to me than my talent for absorbing positive knowledge."*

–Albert Einstein

Chapter Seven
THE FIVE FUNCTIONS
OF YOUR MIND

The more wisdom you receive about your mind, the closer you come to achieving Cosmic Consciousness. In this chapter and the next, you learn yet more about the nature of mind.

The value of mind depends upon how it is used. Mind, on its own, is neither your enemy nor your friend. You can cultivate it to be a friend or you can make it an enemy. It is up to you. YOU stand behind your mind. Master your mind and use it as the superlative instrument it is designed to be, and it becomes the means through which you accomplish great achievements. Mind is an instrument for thinking. For those who have lost control, the mind runs wild.

You may tell your mind to stop obsessing about something, and then it goes right on obsessing even more. Have you ever wanted to sleep but your restless mind kept you awake? You say, "Stop" to your mind but it continued right on buzzing. It may seem that your mind isn't listening to you and you can't seem to do anything about it.

Why?

Because you have allowed your mind to direct you, rather than you directing it.

Think of the predicament that you would be in if your hands and feet behaved like that. Mind is far more powerful than your hands and feet could ever be. You must learn to use your mind just like you use your hands and feet. You exert perfect control over your hands and feet, and they work for you rather than against you. You must get your mind under similar control.

Understanding the five main functions of mental activities helps. The Five Functions are Right Knowledge, Wrong Knowledge, Imagination, Sleep and Memory. Each acts upon and interrelates to the others.

THE FIVE MAIN FUNCTIONS OF MIND

Right Knowledge
Wrong Knowledge
Imagination
Sleep
Memory

RIGHT KNOWLEDGE: The Theory of Positivity

"Two things inspire me to awe...the starry heavens above and the moral universe within."

-Albert Einstein

The Center of Right Knowledge innately and intuitively knows what is right; what is true. Used correctly, it is a searchlight of truth. Wherever it is focused becomes immediately clear to you. Right thinking is a most remarkable mental faculty. When you know how to use it, Right Knowledge will be instinctively revealed. Conversely, not knowing how to use Right Knowledge, you will often be wrong at best 50% of the time. Right Knowledge brings optimism and happiness.

You know that you are using Right Knowledge when you think and do the right thing even if nobody is watching.

WRONG KNOWLEDGE: The Theory of Negativity

"Only two things are infinite, the universe and human stupidity, and I'm not sure about the former."

-Albert Einstein

Be aware, Wrong Knowledge accepts what is untrue as being true. When the mind's mode is of Wrong Knowledge, whatever you choose will be the wrong choice; whatever you decide will be the wrong decision. Further, when you are focused in the wrong, the mind tends to find wrong in everything. This is the basis of pessimism. For some, there are gradients in between Right and Wrong Knowledge. Such minds are sometimes right and sometimes wrong.

As you observe people, you will note that those who use Wrong

Knowledge rather than Right Knowledge, suffer. Direct yourself towards Right Knowledge.

IMAGINATION: The Theory of Serendipity

"I am enough of an artist to draw freely upon my imagination. Imagination is more important than knowledge. Knowledge is limited. Imagination encircles the world."

-Albert Einstein

The third main function of mind is the Center of Imagination. Imagination is your creative function of mind. It is very powerful. All that is beautiful originates in the Imagination, such as: art, music, dance, inventiveness, breakthroughs in science and enlightenment experiences. Mozart's whole compositions came to him in a "flash of a dream" as he took his evening walk. Likewise, everything that is ugly also comes equally through the Imagination.

If Imagination is used in the wrong way, it can be very harmful.

Imagination forms pictures in the mind and transforms the unreal to the real. Some say that when mind energizes imagined images, a matrix in space is formed which starts a process of direct creation or manifestation.

Recognize Imagination as a great mental power and be careful to use it correctly.

Creativity

Dehydrated thoughts,
Saltine crackers in the desert,
Ideas gone dry,
Scattered spinning in lost wind,
Settling like dust.

And each is a seed that any instant,
Blooms tender in the wastelands.
What a wonderful idea!
(It grows on you.)

-Shelley Stockwell

SLEEP: ZZZ Theory
"There is nothing like a dream to create the future."

–Victor Hugo

How nice it is to let things go for some moments of time.

The fourth main function of mind is the Center of Sleep. Sleep is beautiful and life giving. Dreams appear in lighter stages of sleep. Dreams are powerful tools that expand consciousness. They help resolve conflicts, inspire solutions, refresh thoughts and offer new approaches to life. One way to tell if some one is dreaming is to observe their rapid eye movements under closed lids (REM Sleep).

In the deeper sleep, brain activity slows down so the body rejuvenates. One third of your life is spent in this natural shift in consciousness.

Here, your body's power is restored and stress is cleansed. Stress causes your adrenal glands to release the hormone cortisol, which, over time can damage brain cells and shrink your hippocampus which regulates learning and memory. Sleep lowers cortisol, freeing your hippocampus to learn and remember.

Primates eat every two hours and sleep afterwards. Our ancestors did the same. Night was a more dangerous time for food foraging, so humans began to sleep at night and stay awake and hunt in the day. Now we dream in two-hour cycles and during the day we move in and out of subtle brain wave shifts every two hours. Have you ever noticed how sometimes your body becomes still while your brain goes off to scenes in your mind? This timed pattern is a gift from your ancestors.

If you know how to fully utilize Sleep, it can become a source of inspiration. During inspirational Sleep, your consciousness remains awake while you Sleep. At this time, you activate your creativity. The body falls asleep but the witnessing of consciousness remains.

Many innovative solutions have been born in the mind during aware Sleep. Albert Einstein is said to have created many of his famous theories while dreaming.

Sleep

Your time in sleep is blessed,
Time to put your mind at rest.
Free to roam without restraint
Through subject, energy, time and date.
A space to dwell inside your BEING
And be with the spirit of eternal seeing.
When your knit picky brain tries to stand in your way,
The you of your core lets it just fade away.
This is where we all live, where all miracles are true.
It's your daily rebirth for you here on earth.

-Shelley Stockwell

MEMORY: The Theory of Retroactivity
"The only reason for time is so that everything doesn't happen at once."

–Albert Einstein

The Center of Memory is the fifth main function of your mind. Memory is not completely reliable. Memory can be used either correctly of incorrectly. If Memory is misused, it creates confusion. Imagination may enter into Memory, too. You delete things from Memory when you say: "This is what I remember." Much of what you conjure up from out of the past is not real at all, or is distorted.

Instead of being based upon true experiences, Memory may drop that which is disagreeable and hang on to that which is agreeable or vice versa.

To achieve accurate Memory, you must be totally honest with yourself. Only then can Memory serve you well. The secret for achieving "Right Memory" is to accept whatever happened, be it good or bad, without changing it. KNOW IT AS IT IS!

If you correctly remember your past, there is no urge to repeat it in the present. Right Memory helps you live better in the present.

Good hypnoanalysis and past-life regression compels the mind to bring in "Right Memories." When Memories are faced squarely, they lose their power and are dropped. They become "old" business.

You put them in your "trash can" and press "delete." Buried, suppressed Memories can disturb. Remembering often makes them vanish in that instant.

Accurate Memory frees you from past influences in this life and past lives. You transcend all the nonsense that belongs to the past. Far too many think the past was wonderful, the future is going to be terrific, and only the present is mundane. The truth is, only the present is real. There is actually only one way to live; to appreciate the actual life that you are living in the here and now.

Again, the past is but a Memory of what will never happen, while the future may never happen at all. There is only the HERE AND NOW.

Instill the here and now and The Five Main Functions of Mind into your patterns, and you take a quantum leap into higher consciousness. Instill these principles into the mind of your client, and you advance from being a hypnotherapist to being a GREAT hypnotherapist.

Cosmic consciousness moves past linear time into an infinite, timeless and dynamic now.

HYPNOTIC HELPER:
The audiotape, Magnetic Mind Toning, uses a beautiful hypnotic journey to master your mind modes. You can order it using the order form in the back of this book

"A human being is part of a whole, called by us the 'Universe,' a part limited in time and space. He experiences himself, his thoughts and feelings, as something separated from the rest, a kind of optical delusion of his consciousness. This delusion is a kind of prison for us, restricting us to our personal desires and to affection for a few persons near us. Our task must be to free ourselves from this prison by widening our circles of compassion to embrace all living creatures and the whole of nature in its beauty."

-Albert Einstein

Chapter Eight
EXERCISES TO MASTER MIND FUNCTIONS

The Five Main Functions of Mind Merit Further Study
MASTER RIGHT KNOWLEDGE: Learn to accurately assess truth

Right Knowledge is a direct perception of what is true. It is one of your mind's most important functions. With Right Knowledge, your mind is capable of a direct perception of what IS. Even your senses: seeing, hearing, feeling, tasting and smelling can report inaccurately. Senses convey information to the mind but you must question the accuracy of their messages.

Right knowledge arises out of your Inner Self. Direct perception is the mind's function for directly perceiving truth. In other words, mind has the ability to automatically know what is right. In this mental phenomenon, you (as the knower) and the information (as the known) meet directly. In this intimacy of perception, truth is directly conveyed to the mind. You will learn more about transcendent direct perception in Chapter 19: *Your Glorious Immortality.*

MASTER WRONG KNOWLEDGE: Put aside prejudices

We contribute to the mind's faculty of Wrong Knowledge with our prejudices. Prejudice thinks for us before we even start to think. Pre-judging interferes with your instinctive knowing of what is right. To counteract this and acquire Right Knowledge, you must put aside your prejudices. Do this continuously. Ever-repressed prejudices arise anew unless they are kept under surveillance. Only then will you be freed from Wrong Knowledge.

The Dalai Lama is known by Tibetan Buddhists as a reincarnation of the "God of Compassion." This is how he masters wrong thinking every day. Try it and notice how you become more peaceful and compassionate:

Sit quietly with your eyes closed. Relax and be aware. To your left, visualize your self in a moment of impatience. See it with your inner vision. It is OK to employ your imagination. You can imagine how you look and sound to others when you are impatient. What does your face and body language look like? Now, visualize the right side of yourself being patient. Notice how calm and relaxed your patient self is. How do you appear and sound to yourself and others as your patient self? To the right side of your minds eye, visualize and imagine yourself joyous. Become one with that happiness. Know how others see you when you are happy.

Now, on your left side, imagine and visualize yourself as depressed. Be aware of gloom you emit and how that feels. Continue witnessing all seemingly negative and positive attitudes and behaviors. See yourself jealous on the left and glad for someone else's success on the right. See yourself bigoted on the left and then all embracing on the right.

Mean then kind.
Stupid then brilliant.
Clumsy then graceful.
Self-abusive then self-respecting.

As you continue, you become familiar with all the you's on the left. What would you be like without all the you's on the right?
Now, see yourself only as all the you's on the right. Imagine how you would be if none of those on the left had ever appeared.

The Dalai Lama says that when you see your negative self, you will be so disgusted, that you automatically stay positive. Eventually you become exclusively positive. Use the Dalai Lama's technique to master Right Thinking.

MASTER IMAGINATION: Be careful of the words you use

Imagination operates through words. Words produce mental images so powerful they can deceive you. Your Imagination may come to believe that what is not so, is so. If you hypnotize a person and suggest a hallucination, that image appears to the subject's mind as real. Hypnosis is an excellent way to train the mind to accept ideas you want to accept. Conversely, if you accept ideas you don't want to accept, you must reject or reframe those ideas.

Every hypnotist knows the power of words. We all use words so continuously, that we often forget their power. In truth, words are "triggers to action." We have become conditioned to respond to words, frequently without noticing what we are responding to. The words spoken at the right time, can move the world: Buddha's did, Jesus' did, and even Hitler's did.

Imagination must be understood because it is very susceptible and influenced by the words of others. Others teach words, and through words many prejudices are born. Through words, beliefs, myths, illusions, and everything true and false, are stimulated in the Imagination. One must be very cautious of words, for it is common for them to lead you to Wrong Knowledge rather than to Right Knowledge. Some psychics, ministers, and misled therapists specialize "in spirit releasement." Busting "icky" entities that they "suggest" are glommed on to you. They then go to elaborate lengths and high fees to get the "ickies" off your back. Powerful suggestions that frighten and confuse, plant "false memories" that become your reality. Beware of words you accept. You must learn to separate fact from fancy.

MASTER MINDFUL SLEEP: Learn to be mindful of everything you do

For the ordinary mind, deep Sleep largely frees awareness; so you are largely unconscious. But, for the exceptional mind, deep sleep provides a very special state in which you Sleep with awareness. SLEEPING WITH AWARENESS IS ONE OF THE GREAT GOALS OF COSMIC CONSCIOUSNESS. To become aware while you Sleep, you must first learn to be more aware while you are awake; then learn to be aware while you dream. Only if you succeed with the waking state awareness can you master the dreaming state of mind. You'll be able to succeed in the deep Sleep-state. Experiment with awareness and you begin to control your Center of Sleep. Here are six steps you can use to train your mind to dream mindfully:

MINDFUL FOCUS ONE: Wakeful Walking

First, be aware while walking. Don't just walk automatically. Be alert to every movement and action your arms and legs make in walking. Notice muscles rippling under the surface of YOUR legs, feel the way your feet fall upon the ground. Notice your spine, your neck. Be easy and let your walking become a conscious experience of who is doing the walking!

MINDFUL FOCUS TWO: Eat with Reverence

Next, while you eat, become consciously aware of everything; the taste of the food in your mouth, the feeling of the chewing, the way you swallow and the path your food takes. Note how fluids greet food. Notice how you take it in, break it down and absorb from it, its life force. Make eating and drinking a conscious experience.

Who is it who is doing the eating and drinking?

MINDFUL FOCUS THREE: Conscious Breath

Next, take your conscious awareness to your breath. Experience it fully.

Who is it who is doing the breathing?

MINDFUL FOCUS FOUR: Sound Advice

Whatever you hear, notice. Notice fully all sound both inside and outside of your body.

Who is hearing?

Be fully mindful as you speak. Note how you create sound.

Who is doing the talking?

MINDFUL FOCUS FIVE: All Ways Aware

Become aware of whatever you do. Notice how you brush your teeth, shower, comb your hair and put on your clothes. Consciously hug, kiss, make love. Notice yourself driving, cooking, eating, digesting and eliminating. Do each with consciousness. Whatever you do, become alert to the experience.

MINDFUL FOCUS SIX: Mindful Dreaming

Then, in the night, while you are falling asleep, remain aware. Various thoughts of the day will pass through your mind. Watch these. **Remain alert and try to fall asleep with awareness. It may not be easy because of your old mental habits of falling asleep. But if you persist, you will come to sleep and awareness simultaneously. When you do this, you'll experience a transition into higher realms of consciousness.**

It is a very precious moment when you become aware of when the waking state goes and the sleeping state comes. In that neutral moment, just between waking and sleeping, old habits of the mind drop away and you soar upward in consciousness. In that moment, you become aware of your true nature. You'll learn more about controlling your dreams in Chapter 15: *What your Dreams Have To Say.*

MASTER MEMORY: Become aware that Memories can be distorted and that you can remove the distortion

"The intuitive mind is a sacred gift and the rational mind a faithful servant. Society honors the servant and forgets the gift."

—Albert Einstein

Do not allow your Memories of life in the past to rule your life in the present. Learn from them, but be their master. As you gain mastery over Memory, you gain a skill to drop your Memories whenever you please.

Dropping Memories does not mean that you will stop remembering. Dropping Memories simply means that you will drop their constant interference and intrusion into your daily life.

When you need a Memory, you will be able to bring it back into focus. When you do not need the Memory, you will just let it be there silently, rather than come up noisily and uninvited.

*"Don't worry about your problems with mathematics,
I assure you mine are far greater."*

–Albert Einstein

Chapter Nine
HOW TO ACHIEVE
A PEACEFUL MIND

S erenity is always there for you, yet how many people never have it? Serenity is a choice, yet many insist on creating a constant state of mental turmoil and disturbance. In this chapter, Buddha gives you some useful tips on how to have a peaceful mind. Can you imagine anyone more qualified to tell you how to have a peaceful mind than Buddha?

Buddha's disciples once asked: *"Master, how can we attain inner peace like you have? You are always so happy. How can we likewise be so happy?"*

Buddha answered: *"Happiness is a state of mind. It is an attitude. If you are unhappy, just change your attitude and become happy. It is far easier to be happy than it is to be unhappy, for happiness is your true nature. When you are happy, you obtain a peaceful mind."*

Just changing your attitude is what Buddha says. Yet, for a mind not under control by SELF, changing an attitude can be one of the most difficult things in the world. However, when YOU are in control, changing your attitude is as easy as playing the flip side of an audio cassette tape.

Buddha's sutra helps you obtain a peaceful mind. He says: *"The mind becomes tranquil by cultivating attitudes of friendliness toward the happy, compassion toward the miserable, joy toward the virtuous and indifference toward the evil."* Let's consider his directives one by one.

FIRST
"Cultivate Attitudes of Friendliness Toward the Happy"

On the surface, an attitude of friendliness toward a happy person seems easy, but it is not always so. A happy person is successful and the uncontrolled mind may feel jealous of their success. Jealousy says that somehow his or her success and happiness should be yours, not theirs.

Do you feel friendly towards a successful and/or happy person? Have you pretended you did but deep inside you were envious? Change envy if you want a peaceful mind. To truly obtain a tranquil mind, you must become a master of your mind rather than having your mind master you. Buddha says to obtain peace of mind, which leads to mental control: *"Just change your attitude."*

To change your attitude about the happiness and/or success of another, you must come to appreciate that happiness is not a commodity. Happiness is not something which, if someone else gets it, you cannot have it. The whole of life is actually a celebration of billions of happinesses happening all over the universe. If you have an attitude of jealousy, you will be miserable, in a constant hell. You will be in a hell while elsewhere heaven awaits you.

If somebody is happy, what comes first to your mind? Does happiness seem to be taken from you, as if they won and you lost? Do you think somehow that they cheated you?

Change your attitude! Happiness is not a competition. Then, you create heaven from a hell you created in the first place. If somebody is happy, it doesn't mean that you cannot be happy. Happiness exists in an infinite quantity; nobody has ever been able to exhaust it.

Happiness is there just for the taking. Learn how to dip into the cornucopia of the Universe. Create abundance in your life by using the power of your creative mind.

To be peaceful, BYPASS all the jealousy and envy stuff, and when somebody is successful and happy, feel friendly towards them. This wisdom will flip-flop your attitude completely and lead you towards tranquility for yourself. A tranquil mind is a mind under control.

Open a door towards happiness, for, if you can feel friendly towards someone who is happy, you immediately start sharing the happiness. This changing of unfriendliness to an attitude of friendliness towards those who are happy, is a great step forward in obtaining a peaceful mind.

SECOND
"Cultivate an Attitude of Compassion Toward the Miserable"

Friendliness means you create a situation in which you would like to be the same as the other person. Compassion means that you would like to help someone who has fallen from happiness regain their happiness. Compassion is totally different from sympathy. Compassion means you would like to help the other from their misery without allowing their misery to become your misery. Compassion has a *feeling tone* about it; of remaining aloof, while at the same time being attentive.

There is an important lesson here. Misery is an attitude. Even a poor man can be happy and once he is happy, many things start falling in line. Soon, he may not be a poor man. How can someone be poor when he is happy? When you are happy, the whole world participates with you. When you are unhappy, everything goes wrong. This is the dynamics of mind. It is a self-defeating system. This is why Buddha tells you to become master of your attitudes.

THIRD
"Cultivate Joy Towards the Virtuous"

Your mind is suspicious of virtue. When you feel somebody is virtuous, do you think that they must be deceiving you? Does your mind conjure up the attitude: How can anybody be more virtuous than I? When somebody is virtuous, do you start searching for faults? Do you try to bring them down? Buddha says change this attitude. Instead, cultivate Joy towards the virtuous. If you criticize a virtuous person, deep down you are criticizing virtue. Then, before long you believe that virtue is impossible in this world. An uncontrolled mind may move on to hurtful behavior. A mind critical of virtue says: *"Nobody is virtuous, so why be virtuous?"* Much good is lost by this attitude. So Buddha says, change your attitude towards the virtuous and you will obtain a peaceful mind. Virtue is real, accessible and terrific.

FOUR
"Cultivate Indifference Towards Evil"

Evil is the negative side of good.

The mind gravitates towards the negative.

"No" let's you discount information rather than go through the effort of understanding and/or accepting information. It is easier to say "no" than it is to say "yes."

Whenever you say "No," you harm yourself. "No" is self-destructive and makes peace of mind impossible. Buddha says you must affirm the positive to obtain a peaceful mind. He says you advance to a higher consciousness only if you are joyful towards the virtuous (good) and indifferent toward evil. This reverses common attitudes.

It's tempting for the uncontrolled mind to condemn evil. Why not condemn evil? If you condemn evil, you pay too much attention to evil. And, you become attuned (become like) that to which you pay attention. In other words, you become addicted with wrong. And, to be wrong causes a very unpeaceful mind.

Shakespeare said: *"The lady protesteth too much."* If you are overly attentive to evil, negative, or wrong knowledge, you tend to head towards evil, negativity and wrong knowledge. To resist negativity, become indifferent to it. Such is Cosmic Wisdom.

Being indifferent to evil drops evil from your nature.

Jesus says, "Judge ye not."

"Resist not evil." Buddha says.

"Be indifferent," I say "and strive for positive neutrality in all situations."

The famous French psychologist, Emil Coué, discovered a law of human behavior, which he called: *"The Law of Reverse Effort."* which says, that if you are too much against something, you will become a victim of it. Action follows your attention.

Buddha uses four ways to obtain a peaceful mind: *"Change your attitude about happiness, miserableness, virtue and evil."*

Reflect on the way you felt when you felt peaceful with yourself. Mentally be there and relive that time.

Sit quietly and experience how you feel. Direct your attention towards how you breathe when peaceful. Completely program your breath for right now so you can breathe like that anytime you want. Remember, the rhythm of that peaceful breathing. Whenever you wish to return to this serene state of mind, just breathe in that exact manner. Quickly, you will be there.

If your mind is not tranquil, try this:

Start by exhaling all your breath. Exhale as completely as you can. With the throwing out of your breath, your mood of anxiety will be thrown out likewise, because breathing is basic. To aid in fully expelling your breath, pull your belly in, and for a few seconds, don't inhale. Then, inhale deeply until your lungs are completely full. Then stop again and hold the breath in for a few seconds. The gap between the "in" breath and the "out" breath should be the same. For example, if you retain the out breath for three seconds, likewise retain the in breath for three seconds. Continue this method of controlled breathing for a little while, exhaling and inhaling totally in a soothing rhythm.

Within minutes, you will feel changes. Anxiety will evaporate, and in its place, your mind will be peaceful. Obtaining a peaceful mind is to become master of your mind. Mastering your mind is to become a MASTERMIND. When you are a MASTERMIND, you are well on your way to Cosmic Consciousness.

Through mind, consciousness is known.

*"Gravitation can not be held responsible
for people falling in love."*

-Albert Einstein

Chapter Ten
MASTERING DESIRE

E arthly desires can frustrate, disturb and keep you clinging to lower consciousness. Mastering Desire gives a boost to achieving Cosmic Consciousness.

Constant desiring makes the mind restless and discontented. Desirelessness, on the other hand, makes the mind happy and contented. End the nagging search to find happiness outside of yourself. Master your desires rather than being mastered by them and you obtain a peaceful mind. A peaceful mind is nicely free from desires.

How do you do this?
Step One:

The first step to mastering desires: Recognize that your real source of happiness is found *inside* of yourself rather than *outside* of yourself.

Step Two:

Look within to your real source of happiness and you discover your SELF. Your true self will tell you that real happiness is your true nature. Real happiness emanates from your inner self.

Desires place demands that call to be satisfied. We often satisfy such desires and demands with self-indulgent or sensuous pleasures. We seek fulfillment externally through our senses and with things. We seem satisfied, but not for long. Very soon, desire arises again and demands even greater quantities of satisfaction. The quest for questing distorts your perception of the source of real happiness. External rewards create a vicious circle.

If you persist in craving more things and more often, habits and/or addictions follow. Persistent habits form a "mental set," such as a program in a computer. Once you key it in, it plays on its own and then commands you rather than you commanding it. In other words, desires often become involuntary acts (habits of behavior). To drop automatic behavior you have to change them into voluntary acts so you can deal with them.

You hope that desire and habit will bring you satisfaction. Satisfaction is good. But, external desires lower your awareness (consciousness) of your real SELF. To move towards the happiness that is your true nature, follow these five directives:

1. Consciously think of your mind mastering desires rather than adhering unconsciously to old habits or desires.

2. Appreciate that nothing stops you from enjoying life to the fullest. Your real source of happiness is far deeper than superficial happiness you get questing to satisfy worldly desire. Then you are free to be happy!

3. Appreciate that when your mind is free of desires rather than cluttered up trying to figure out how to satisfy them, you are much happier.

4. Accept that the real source of your happiness is found in your inner world (inside yourself) rather than in the outer world (outside yourself).

5. Discover your SELF, which dwells within your inner world. When you do, you embrace your true nature, which is so complete, you need desire nothing further. YOU HAVE IT ALL .

It is easy to understand these steps, but it takes conscious effort to own them. Old habits resist change. Change them you must if you would discover your true nature and achieve a peaceful mind.

To master desire, don't struggle against your right nature. Effort must be made without effort. That is why hypnosis is so effective. As you simply relax and drop off into a reverie state, suggestions change your mind effortlessly.

Don't fight yourself. Over-ride desires the undisciplined mind conjures as your nature. Fighting yourself, is a losing battle. Who is going to win and who will lose? You are both sides. There is no great division between your so-called higher self and lower self. In truth, there is nothing higher or lower about you. You are both; there is no need to divide yourself.

Fight FOR your nature. You accumulate many limiting habits during the course of your life. Because of these, your true nature cannot move spontaneously. These habits have to be changed, but they are only habits. They may seem like your nature because you are addicted to them, but the truth is, they are not you.

This distinction has to be clearly understood; otherwise you can misinterpret these instructions. The basic purpose for mastering desires is to keep external things that bring no real happiness under control. Know the YOU within brings you happiness overflowing.

These are directions, not laws. They are not to be followed like an obsession. They are simply to be understood so that their meaning is carried into your life, both physically and mentally. Then you will achieve mastery over your desires, which is really mastery over yourself. Desirelessness is a direction, a focal point. Pursue mastering desires as an obsession and you start killing all desires. On the surface, it seems logical to diligently seek no desire to master desire. If you emphatically stop all desiring, you will be lifeless. You will be committing inner suicide. Desires are the flow of life energy. DESIRELESSNESS IS TO BE ACHIEVED WITH MORE LIFE, NOT LESS. Wrongly used, mastering desires can suppress your life. Rightly used, it gives you boundless life.

When you are filled with overflowing energy, it leads you into many desires. Since a desire is only energy, you can handle it one of two ways. One, drop your desire while allowing the energy to remain. Or two, drop the level of your energy, which will cause the desire to disperse. In doing this, you achieve a state in which you master your desires and are still filled with energy.

Just follow this rule: DON'T SUPPRESS ENERGY... TRANSCEND DESIRE.

Recognize that real happiness comes to you from inside yourself rather than from outside yourself. Use conscious effort to drop desire from your mind and cease any endless search for happiness from earthly pleasures. Happiness outside is only a mirror reflecting your inner happiness. You narrow your happiness potential if you do not recognize the tremendous happiness potential inside yourself. Become aware of your innate happiness potential and you will master desire.

To help you do this, close your eyes and look within. Where does your pleasure come from? See the truth about pleasure. Let your perception be accurate.

It is from this moment pleasure comes. This moment is precious to mastering your mind. This glorious awareness of your source of happiness evokes a quantum leap into your true nature. In this, you discover your SELF and automatically stop hankering for outside pleasures. All the frustration you felt yearning for unfulfilled desires wither away on its own and you become master of desire.

FOR TRUE HAPPINESS, CONSCIOUS EFFORT IS NEEDED. WHENEVER YOU FEEL A MOMENT OF PLEASURE, BECOME A WITNESS TO THE SITUATION.

Becoming master of your desires is a giant step along the way in your search for Cosmic Consciousness.

HYPNOTIC HELPER:
Our audiotape, The Violet Flame, will help you expand into a state of reverie. You can order it in the back of this book.

*"The most incomprehensible thing about
the universe is that it is incomprehensible."*

-Albert Einstein

Chapter Eleven

ADVANCING YOUR CONSCIOUSNESS

Your search for cosmic Consciousness requires two things. One, that you understand its nature: a cosmic staircase of Unconscious Consciousness, Simple Consciousness, Animal Consciousness, Self-Consciousness and Cosmic Consciousness. Everything in the Universe is sentient. That is, everything is conscious to the degree of being what it IS.

Two, Cosmic Consciousness requires that you really understand the nature of your mind. Both interrelate and belong to your immortality.

Understand your true nature. In relation to yourself, you are an individual SELF-Consciousness. To advance, you must master your mind and KNOW yourself and that your SELF is in harmony with all that IS. This is direct knowing. This is Direct Perception.

With Cosmic Consciousness, you advance from knowledge to KNOWING or wisdom. There is a difference between and wisdom and knowledge. Someone who has learned from others has knowledge stored within his memory. Ask that person a new question and they will be at a loss to answer it. They only give answers they have been told the answer to. This is the difference between the educated person and the sage. Most educated people repeat what they have learned, while the sage uses consciousness to bring in the answer. The wisdom of a sage is directly related to Cosmic Consciousness.

The following four processes will help you develop wisdom:
1. Use your mind for reasoning, optimism, reflection and clarity.
2. Unclutter your mind and become *silent.* Invite in KNOWING.
3. Recognize your immortality.
4. Employ faith, effort, recollection, concentration and discrimination.

STEP 1
Use Your Mind for Reasoning, Optimism, Reflection and Clarity

Your attitudes create and direct thoughts. Each thought carries its own energy. If you allow thoughts uncontrolled, you become possessed by them rather than mastering them. Direct your mind toward positive reasoning and you practice thinking. Thinking is a capacity; thoughts are not. *Thinking is something you have to learn for yourself.*

Use thoughts positively. Positive reasoning frees a cluttered mind from disturbances so you can really think. Be optimistic…accept life with a positive attitude.

Thinking is a quality of your inner being. A really thinking person uses consciousness each time they seek a solution to a problem. You are not presented a problem without a solution.

Stockwell's Tips:

"Do not be timid and squeamish about your actions. All life is an experiment."

-Ralph Waldo Emerson

Think about an unpleasant experience in your life. Tell yourself the story the way that you always have. Now pause and notice how you feel (Pause).
Are you agitated?
Such negative energy does not open you to Cosmic Consciousness.

Now, let's try it again.
This time, tell yourself about the same experience in a new and positive way. Discover the humor. What came from it? What did you learn? Celebrate the experience as a positive force in your life. (Pause) How do you feel now? (Pause)

Congratulations! When you focus on the positive, you begin to advance your consciousness.

Positive reasoning leads to reflection. Reflection provides you with a glimpse of truth. It is only a glimpse of truth; it will come and go, and for a moment the mind is flooded with insight. This glimpse of truth is important because it lets you recognize your possibilities and experience pure thought. It shows that you are heading in the right direction.

STEP 2
Unclutter Your Mind and be Silent

How do you make your mind silent? This happens automatically when you rise above the ceaseless barrage of thoughts not under your control. When your mind is silent, you are *aware of awareness*. In silence, you no longer try to think. Thinking occurs on its own. This is the beginning of KNOWING. In this stage, you come to know yourself personally and start to recognize your true nature.

Stockwell's Tips:

Three Deep Breaths: Up, Up and Away

Notice how you are feeling right now in this moment. Then...

1) Look up at the top of this page and take a deep breath.

2) Look up at the ceiling and take another deep breath.

3) Finally, look up, all the way up, and take a third deep breath.

Notice how much better you feel in this moment.

What's the difference?

You shifted your perception by uplifting your eyes. Chemically, you change your brain signals for up-liftment. Any time you consciously move your eyes upward and bathe yourself with more oxygen, you feel better.

1) Again, look up at the top of the page and take a deep breath.

2) Look up at the ceiling and take another deep breath.

3) Look up, all the way up, and take a third deep breath. This time, touch your thumb to your forefinger on one hand, making the sign of OK.

This symbol serves as your joy anchor.

Think of your mind as a bio computer and you are the programmer. Any time you feel low, take three deep breaths, uplift your focus, and make the OK sign. If you really want to blast yourself into joy, straighten your posture, say "yes" to yourself and laugh (Hee, hee, hah, hah).

STEP 3
Recognize Your Immortality

Enter the silence and you discover your true nature. You'll find yourself thinking more and more about immortality. How little your body has to do with the real nature of yourself. It dawns on you that you are a consciousness independent of the body. That consciousness is not bounded by the three-dimensional space of the physical world. Your consciousness transcends body and lifetimes. Your soul is eternally and perpetually growing.

Memories of other places in time flow up from your subconscious. Remembering them is important for cleansing your mind. Use hypnosis to direct the subconscious to probe memory. Put yourself into a state of mind that allows your mind to drift and form whatever scenarios unfold. Just *witness* adventures flowing out of your subconscious.

Repressed memory causes tensions and makes a noisy mind. When repressions are released, the mind becomes silent. Both the conscious and subconscious phase of mind become silent, and a silent mind is open to Cosmic Consciousness.

With the recognition of your immortality, you will know, and KNOWING is truth.

How to Travel Time

A terrific way to explore your immortality is to take a Time Travel Journey. You can journey with a Past Life Therapist, Hypnotist, use my audio tape "Time Travel" or take yourself through time.

Here's how to do your own journey:

1. Get comfortable in a place where you will not be disturbed.

2. Decide if you want to go to a past life, future life, parallel life or between life. Decide also if you want to explore through time, a relationship: "Why am I attracted to someone?" or "Why do I have such an aversion to someone?" Maybe you want to explore a physical experience: "What is the source of my asthma?" or "Why am I such a great athlete?" You can track an emotion: "Why do I get emotional when I see a fire." You can enrich a talent: "I want to go to a life time where I know all about herbs." If you like, take an open ended journey and go wherever you go.

3. Play some soft music and sit back and relax.

4. Say a blessing/prayer:

"**Bless me on all levels: Physically, mentally, spiritually and emotionally. May all these teachings be for my highest good as I journey to (the past, future, between lives, parallel lives) another place in time. I will not censor, analyze, edit or judge. I allow what I need to know about my immortality to come to me. Help me to release and forgive myself or anyone who treated me with insensitivity and help me embrace all of the lessons and blessings of my journey. Thank you, Amen, Awomen, Ah Life!**"

5. Imagine yourself going down a corridor of time. There are many portals along the path, each one will take you to another place in time. Allow the perfect corridor to beckon you in.

6. Answer these questions with the first thing that comes to your mind; do not censor or analyze. Let the story unfold. Take your time. Don't be concerned if it makes sense or not. Report to yourself whatever you experience.

Are you inside or out?
Alone or with someone?
Are you sitting, standing, or lying down?
Are you warm or cold?
Be aware of your feet (if you have feet) how are they wrapped?
How is your body covered?
Are you male or female?
What is going on?
What happens next?
Where is this place?
What is the date?
Tell yourself about all the highlights of this life time.
How did you die?
After you die, send white light upon you.
What happens when the light shines upon you.
Go to the light.
What did you learn from this lifetime?
How have these lessons affected you in your current lifetime?
Before you return to your here and now, is there anything you need to say to yourself?

When you are ready, return feeling refreshed, invigorated and so glad to be alive."

Write down your experience or record it on a tape player.

STEP 4
Employ Faith, Effort, Recollection, Concentration and Discrimination
Consider each of these in turn:

Faith
Blind faith is something others believe and insist you must believe too. They hand you that belief, then insist that you accept it. That kind of faith has no value in expanding your consciousness. It constricts, rather than expands you.

The faith you need for Cosmic Consciousness uses the Law of Divine Assumption: *believe what you believe without proof that it is*. This faith is in yourself. It is your own creation and you grow into it. Cosmic Consciousness is the faith that accepts all that YOU are as being YOU.

The faith you create for yourself uses your Creative Mind. Your creative mind blends imagination and feeling.

Effort
Put your total bio-energy into BEING. The entire universe is an energy phenomenon and you are part of it.

Recollection
In relation to Cosmic Consciousness, it is important to re-collect or re-remember yourself. Many people remember many things, but continuously forget themselves. Here is a technique you can use to remember yourself: Whatever you do, know and understand that "I am doing the doing."

"It is I who am walking." From your *center of being*, witness the walking. Do not just repeat it in your mind; such means nothing and is not remembrance. What is needed is to become aware that:

"I am walking." "I am eating." "I am talking." "I am listening."
While doing whatever you do, the "I" inside yourself must

always be remembered. This is not self-consciousness. It is consciousness of SELF.

The process is not as easy to master as it sounds. It is easy to remember the object (what is being done) and forget your SELF (who is doing the doing). You might remember yourself (the one doing) and forget the object (what is being done). But to re-collect yourself, you must be aware of the two together. When you can note the object (what is being done) and the doer (who is doing it) you begin to have self-remembrance.

Eventually, self-remembrance will become so much a part of you that it becomes your way of looking at life and relating yourself to life. Even if you succeed in attaining this dual perception of your SELF for only a single moment, you will have had a flash of Cosmic Consciousness. Ah ha; Satori.

Concentration

Enlightenment is a concentrated experiencing of the universe and your relationship to it. Concentrate your attention on the way you unfold and grow. Unfoldment and your focus upon it continuously grows within you. It becomes a 24-hour experience that once started, never stops.

Discrimination

Discrimination allows you to determine how you wish to think and what you want to do. Then, you think and do what you decide. Discrimination means that you are becoming conscious of your consciousness.

Chapter Thirteen of this book presents a "Self-Hypnosis Suggestion Formula" to implant each of these Cosmic Consciousness Concepts into your subconscious mind so that you make them your very own.

HYPNOTIC HELPER:
Shelley Stockwell's audiotape, Time Travel, helps you explore and release repressed memory. It's fun to close your eyes and discover who you were before you were you.

PART THREE
TECHNIQUES TO HELP YOUR SEARCH

"If we knew what we were doing, it would not be called research, would it?"

-Albert Einstein

"All religions, arts and sciences are branches of the same tree. All these aspirations are directed toward ennobling human life, lifting it from the sphere of mere physical existence and leading the individual towards freedom."

-Albert Einstein

Chapter Twelve
SELF-HYPNOSIS REVERIE

Self-Hypnosis is a self-induced state of mind. Western in origin, it is used in many parts of the world under different names.

In the East, Meditation is practiced widely. Self-Hypnosis and Meditation are similar and vastly different. The goal of Self-Hypnosis is to fill your mind with purpose. While the goal of Meditation, (which you will learn in chapter 16: *The Art of Meditation*), is to empty the mind.

Both self-hypnosis and meditation aid you to turn inward and discover the true nature of your SELF, so you harmonize your inner and outer world. Both turn you inward to unfold your divine nature. In Bali, hypnotic trance, practiced in dance rituals and healing is called "Karoahan," which means "God coming."

To accomplish Self-Hypnosis, relax the body, quiet the mind and implant in your subconscious the specific goal you want to accomplish.

In relation to advancing consciousness, self-hypnosis is very helpful. You can use it to give direct suggestions to the subconscious; to behave as you want it to behave. You can request it to advance your consciousness of all that IS. Use this method:

SELF HYPNOSIS REVERIE

Go into your private room alone and close the door. Place a candle on a table in front of a comfortable chair. Dim the lights in the room and light the candle. Take a seat in the chair, relax and stare at the flickering flame of the candle.

Now, take six deep breaths in rapid succession. As you do this breathing, keep your eyes fixed upon the candle flame. With each breath, think to yourself:

"I am becoming more and more comfortable and relaxed."

Place your hands over your ears and gently press in. Now speak out loud to yourself and observe the effect. Speaking out loud to yourself with your ears covered in this manner is a powerful way to present suggestions to yourself. It causes the suggestions to ring through your head. It adds vibration. Because this exercise requires you to close your eyes, you may want to record it and recite along with the audio tape. Or keep your eyes gently open and read the following:

"As I watch the candle flame, my eyelids are becoming heavier and heavier. Soon they will become so heavy my eyes will close. I cannot keep my eyes open any longer. I let my eyes close now. As my eyes close, the muscles around my eyes become so relaxed that I cannot open my eyes no matter how hard I try."

Let these suggestions ring through your head while you stare at the candle. Your eyes will quickly close as the suggestions set in.

"My eyes now close and are so relaxed they will not open."

You will find you actually cannot open your eyes. You have bypassed critical mind. Forget about your eyes now and let these suggestions ring through your head:

"The relaxation from my eyes now flows down over my entire body and I am sinking back, back into this comfortable chair and am relaxing completely from head to toe. I have become totally relaxed all over as I enter into this state of hypnotic reverie."

Continue giving your self-suggestion out loud with your hands remaining pressed over your ears:

"My breaths become deeper and deeper now with every breath I take. Every breath is making me more and more comfortable and relaxed. Relaxed. So relaxed, that I find myself getting sleepy and drifting away into hypnotic reverie."

Rest a moment and give attention to your breathing. Then continue:

"Reverie. Reverie. Wonderful hypnotic reverie. It belongs to the realm of sleep and dreams. Yes. I am becoming sleepy as I drop down deep into this wonderfully comfortable reverie. Every suggestion I give myself is accepted by my subconscious and becomes reality. My conscious mind moves aside and allows my subconscious to come forth to accept the suggestions I give myself...to improve the quality of my life...to advance my consciousness through this wonderful hypnotic reverie.

As my hands drop down from my ears and fall limply into my lap, I fully enter in hypnotic reverie and transform every suggestion I give myself into reality. I give myself suggestions that benefit me in every way. The gates of my subconscious mind open, and I am ready to receive and transform my life. I spiral upwards advancing my consciousness higher and higher, to ever increasing awareness of the Universe. Universal wisdom now comes into me. COME IN. COME IN. COME IN."

Stop speaking to yourself now. THINK your suggestions inside your mind. (Pause)

"I transform my consciousness. The suggestions I give myself become my reality. I am ready. I am ready. Every suggestion I give myself sends me down deeper and deeper into hypnotic reverie." (Pause)

"When I am ready and not before, I return to my wakeful state; refreshed and invigorated and so glad to be alive. One, two, three four, and five! Feeling terrific, yes!

Use SELF-HYPNOSIS REVERIE often. You can combine it with the suggestion formulas in the following chapter. With hypnosis, you master the control of mind. You direct your functions of mind to achieve a peaceful mind and Cosmic Consciousness.

Cosmic Consciousness is entirely a matter of KNOWING. It can happen this very moment, or it can take lifetimes. It's entirely a matter of how aware you are of your knowing.

How Will I Know if I Have Achieved Knowing?

You will experience yourself as peaceful inside. You'll witness your life adventures without getting perpetually and personally in the whirlpools of stuff all about yourself. It is as though somehow you rise above the world. Everything seems somehow clear to you. Self-Hypnosis Reverie advances you on your way toward achieving the joy of KNOWING.

HYPNOTIC HELPER:
Ormond McGill's audiotape, Yoga Nidra/Hypnoyoga is a terrific way to use hypnosis to advance Cosmic Consciousness. You can order it using the order form in the back of this book.

Photo by Jon Nicholas

"The perfect pattern, a divine design. A place you are to fill and no one else can fill, something you are to do, which no one else can do."

-Plato

Chapter Thirteen
AROUSAL FROM SELF-HYPNOSIS REVERIE

Arousal shifts your "mental gears" or energy from subconsciousness to consciousness. Arousal should be performed pleasantly. Giving suggestions to your mind while in hypnosis is like talking to yourself. While in hypnosis, you talk to your subconscious phase of mind. When you are in your wakeful state, you talk to your conscious mind.

FUTURE SUCCESS

Prior to returning to your "room awareness" make an agreement with your subconscious that you will be able to re-enter hypnosis easily and quickly any time you choose.

FORGET ME NOT

If you wish to tuck away your experience into the deeper mind, (amnesia) give yourself that suggestion. Profound effects occur when experiences bypass a questioning critical mind. Your subconscious frequently performs miracles on its own.

"Mentally set" the amnesia by telling yourself that your self-hypnosis session will seem like a dream. And like a dream, it will quickly fade away.

This works wonders.

TIMELY SUGGESTION

You can "mentally set" your mind computer to arouse yourself from the Hypnosis. Suggestions you give yourself while in hypnosis program your subconscious. In the pleasant state of hypnosis your mind amplifies suggestions.

THE COUNT

"Not everything that counts can be counted and not everything that can be counted counts."

—Albert Einstein

Arouse from hypnosis gradually. Usually hypnotists use a counting sequence.

"As I count from 1 to 5, I feel more and more refreshed, invigorated and so glad to be alive. One, two, three, four, five."

Your mind likes logical progressions. Counting provides a "mental set" for arousing on cue and gradually shifting from subconscious to conscious. How fast or slowly you count makes no difference. Your brain computer operates more rapidly than your wagging tongue.

ALL'S WELL THAT ENDS WELL

End your self-hypnosis suggestions with thoughts of well being. Make your arousal pleasant, happy and beneficial. Mentally set your mind for enjoyment.

Always include a positive uplifting suggestion before you come back to room awareness.

"You return to the here and now feeling wonderful in every way."

GENERAL AROUSAL SUGGESTION FORMULA

For your convenience, here is a generalized arousal "suggestion formula" that does the job well:

"It is time to come out of hypnosis now and return to the here and now. Think of awakening. How pleasant is it to be in the reverie state. The very thought of having to come out of it sinks you yet deeper into it. So, I will let you enjoy hypnosis for a few

more moments, as you sink down into it. Go down deeper now, as you wish.

You sink so deeply into hypnosis that when you come back, even the memory of what occurred while you were in hypnosis will be remote, far away and forgotten. Your subconscious mind remembers and automatically puts into effect suggestions that benefit your life. All the helpful suggestions, now make a deep, permanent and lasting impression on your mind.

Now that you know how pleasant and beneficial hypnosis is for you, each time you re-enter hypnosis, you will find it increasingly easy to do. Whenever you wish to be hypnotized, you rapidly drop down into profound hypnosis. And, each time you do so, you go into deeper and deeper levels of hypnosis. This gives you wonderful control over your subconscious mind. All right now, you have rested long enough. It is time to awaken from hypnosis. To make it very easy for you I will count from one to five and by the time I reach the count of FIVE, you'll be back in the here and now."

You can speak in the 1st or 2nd person when presenting suggestion to your subconscious.

"I am getting ready to awaken now. One, two: I am gradually arousing myself from hypnosis. Three, four: I am arousing and stirring about. My eyes are opening. FIVE: I am fully aroused, alert and back in the here and now feeling wonderful and fine!"

HYPNOTIC HELPER:
The audio tape, *Peace and Calm*, teaches you self hypnosis and self love. You can order it using the order form in the back of this book.

"Only one who devotes himself to a cause with his whole strength and soul can be a true master. For this reason, mastery demands all of a person."

-Albert Einstein

Chapter Fourteen
MASTERMIND HYPNOTHERAPY

Helping Others Advance to Cosmic Consciousness

Hypnosis heals the hypnotized and the hypnotist. Mastermind Hypnotherapy is simple, direct and all-inclusive. It strengthens your personality and lets you master your mind and advance consciousness. Hypnotic suggestions are just words. How can just words have such power?

We are so accustomed to using words that often we forget their real significance. Words offer mind-to-mind communication among all people. Words are "conditioned responses" that affect us without our even thinking that they do. Words effect us spontaneously. Words are "triggers to action." But, never forget that behind the energy of your words stands YOU.

The four specific suggestion formulas for *Mastermind Hypnotherapy* are astoundingly powerful. Use each while your mind is in the super-receptive state of hypnotic reverie and you will bypass your critical thought, which sometimes says "you can't." This way you'll establish selective thinking that affirms that YOU are a limitless miracle.

This hypnotic trance works whether your eyes are open or closed, so long as your mind is set to receive. Your subconscious mind directs your thinking. You'll take these suggestions in fully when you turn the process over to SELF.

You can have a hypnotist or special friend read the formula to you. Or, you can read it to yourself. In your reverie, you may not be in a state of mind to repeat a lengthy dissertation, so you could record each suggestion formula and play the tape back to yourself. You can give these suggestions to your hypnotized clients and friends too. Begin with this introduction:

"I open my eyes now and read out loud to myself the suggestion formula which goes deeply into my subconscious and becomes my reality. As I open my eyes, I read and recite the suggestions. They continually deepen my hypnotic reverie."

Then, place hands cupped over your ears, and read out loud whatever suggestion formula you have placed before yourself. WHEN COMPLETED, drop your hands from your ears to your lap, close your eyes and relax several moments. Allow the suggestions to sink in. Then arouse from hypnosis.

SUGGESTION FORMULA FOR CONTROLLING YOUR MIND
"Problems cannot be solved at the same level of awareness that created them."

–Albert Einstein

Induce hypnosis and present this to the subconscious mind:

"You are keenly aware of all self talk.
You have perfect control over your mind. Your control over your mind lifts you to heights of genius. You instinctively make your mind think what you want it to think. You have automatic control of your mind. Your mind thinks what you want it to think.
You instinctively make your mind think when you want it to think and to stop thinking when you want it to stop thinking. You have absolute control over your mind.
Your mind, is absolutely under your control. Your thoughts are orderly and disciplined. You turn your mind on and off at will. You instinctively witness your thoughts. You witness thoughts as you think them. Your entire perception is that of becoming a witness to your thoughts.
Your perfect control over your mind is your very own. Your subconscious and superconscious mind makes this your reality."

Repeat this "suggestion formula" three times. Repetition is the driving force of successful suggestions. Then, arouse from the hypnosis feeling wonderful. Use only one specific suggestion formula during each session. The mind works best when it is not over-burdened.

SUGGESTIONS FOR YOUR FUNCTIONS OF MIND

Your subconscious knows each of these five mental functions intimately. These suggestions stimulate them into action:

"Your mind has five main functions: a Center of Right Knowledge, Wrong Knowledge, Imagination, Sleep and Memory. You use these functions perfectly to benefit your life.

Your mind automatically brings in Right Knowledge. You make the right decisions. You do the right thing. Always turn your mind in the direction of Right Knowledge. Right Knowledge is the way you use your mind.

You turn away from and reject Wrong Knowledge. You say good kind and loving things to yourself. Right Knowledge completely overwhelms and vanishes Wrong Knowledge. Wrong Knowledge is now forever replaced by Right Knowledge. From this time on, you function from your Center of Right Knowledge. You quickly and easily change any negative to positive.

Your Imagination creates wonderful and beautiful things. Your Imagination is very powerful and it creates a bountiful life for you. You have perfect control over your Imagination and you use it to benefit your life in every way.

You use the power of Sleep to benefit you. You sleep soundly and well and Sleep refreshes and revitalizes you. Sleep is healthful in every way. Sleep benefits you in every way. As you Sleep, the quality of your Sleep changes, as you become a witness or your consciousness. Your body benefits from Sleep, making you well, rested and happy. While your body sleeps, you witness your consciousness. During Sleep you advance your control over your mind. You use your mind as the superb instrument it is.

You use your Memory accurately. You remember and recall things perfectly. Your Memory functions accurately. Your Memory functions perfectly. Your Memory is precise and you remember things as they actually are. You are free from disturbing Memory. Past Memories have no influence over you. You live fully in the here and now.

Each of these five functions of mind is completely under

your control. You use each function of mind to benefit your life in every way. The functions of your mind are at your command. Right Knowledge is always yours. You automatically reject Wrong Knowledge. Your Imagination is creative and it creates wonderful and beautiful things. Sleep brings you perfect rest and well being. While your body sleeps, your consciousness advances your control over your mind. Your Memory functions perfectly. You use your memories to aid you to live life fully in the here and now. All of these suggestions go deep into your subconscious and become your reality; they become your way of life. The power over Knowledge, Imagination, Sleep, and Memory is your very own!"

Note: Repeat this entire "suggestion formula" to yourself or your client three times in succession, ending with...

"You now perfectly control your Mind Functions. This correct use of your mind benefits you in every way."

Arouse from hypnosis reverie.

SUGGESTION FORMULA FOR MASTERING DESIRE

Master desire and you recognize the source of real happiness. This produces a quantum leap in awareness and leads to bliss and Cosmic Consciousness.

Induce hypnosis for yourself or another:

"You are the master of your desires. You know that your true source of happiness originates inside yourself. You are filled with energy to live life fully and to the hilt. Your desires are good ones that benefit you in every way.

You discover your inner SELF. The source of your happiness comes from inside you. Knowing where your real happiness comes from gives you perfect mastery over desire. You have fun with desire. You can play games or not play games with desire, for you have mastered your desires.

Having perfect control let's you enjoy whatever you want. Desire is just a game of fun you play in your earth walk. As master of your desire, happiness flows through you at all times and you radiate happiness to others.

You are filled with boundless energy and your energy makes you the complete master of your desires. Whenever you want anything, you witness it as a thing apart, and you then decide whether or not you wish to satisfy the desire.

Desire is entirely under your own control. You are the master of your desires. You achieve neutrality over desire and this makes you the master. You are aware of your true nature. You know that your real happiness emanates from inside yourself and you already have it ALL. In knowing that your inner SELF is your real source of happiness, desire has completely lost control over you. You are the master of your SELF.

You discover your SELF. Your true happiness comes from deep inside you. Knowing this has given you perfect control. You are master of your desires. Your mastery gives you control over all habits. You enjoy things because you want to enjoy them, not because a habit makes you enjoy it.

When you do not want a habit, you simply let it go. It is easy, for in mastering desire you have absolute control over your habits. You master any and all habits.

You know the real source of happiness. You have perfect control of all earthly desire. You appreciate and enjoy life to the fullest. Your real happiness is found within yourself.

It feels so good to be the master of desire. It makes your mind free and happy.

You know your SELF who dwells in your inner world. You know that you are complete in every way. YOU HAVE IT ALL ALREADY! These suggestions for mastering your desire go directly into your subconscious mind and become your very own, making you the master of all desire for your SELF. This is your source of real happiness."

Repeat this entire "suggestion formula" three times in succession to yourself or client and then arouse from hypnosis

SUGGESTION FORMULA FOR ADVANCING YOUR CONSCIOUSNESS

This is a lengthy suggestion formula. One time through is

sufficient per session. Induce hypnosis and present your subconscious this hypnotic reverie:

"You now expand your consciousness in every way. Know your SELF as an individual consciousness. You are the only one precisely like yourself in the entire universe. You know your true nature. You are increasingly conscious of your consciousness with every breath you take.

You are more and more aware of your true nature with every breath you take. You recognize yourself as consciousness. You recognize yourself as a consciousness. In becoming conscious of your consciousness, you advance your consciousness. Your consciousness is advancing to Cosmic Consciousness in which you recognize your true nature as an immortal being in complete harmony with the universe.

Cosmic Consciousness floods your mind like a bright light and all things become clear to you. Flashes of Cosmic Consciousness come into you. These flashes of KNOWING bring in the truth about all that IS. You know more and more from this time forward. Your consciousness is advancing. You attain Cosmic Consciousness.

As your consciousness advances, your mind becomes silent and uncluttered. KNOWING comes into your mind with crystal clarity.

More and more you recognize your immortality, and identify more and more with your essence.

Your mind is clear like crystal. You think with crystal clarity. You have direct perception of truth and what IS. What you think flows into you with truth and clarity. Your mind functions with perfection.

Your reasoning is positive and optimistic. Your thoughts are filled with energy and produce energy that you direct for your highest good. You attain Cosmic Consciousness. Your intellect and your ability to think with crystal clarity, lets you know instinctively what is truth. Your mind is boundless. You clearly answer all questions for yourself and others through direct perception. You are advancing to Cosmic Consciousness.

The power of reflection brings you glimpses of the truth. You reflect upon the truth. Experiencing truthful reflection advances your consciousness more and more.

You automatically clear your mind of thoughts anytime you please. It is easy for you to do. Your mind becomes silent under your control. More and more you KNOW about your true nature. You understand your immortal nature in an ever-increasing expansion of your consciousness.

Memories of your past, future and parallel lives flow into your mind. Each brings up information that is valuable to you. You enjoy these as entertainment. You face these memories clearly and remove their influence over your current life. This gives you perfect peace of mind.

Your advancement to Cosmic Consciousness, brings you faith in yourself. You are filled with bioenergy. This energy advances your consciousness more and more.

You develop self-remembrance. In everything you do, you witness yourself doing it and KNOW that you are the one who is doing whatever you do. Your self-awareness advances your consciousness. When you walk, you know it is YOU who is walking. When you eat, you know it is YOU who is eating. When you talk, you know it is YOU who is talking. With everything you do, YOU have self-remembrance that YOU are the doer.

Your mind concentrates upon whatever you turn your attention to. This quality of concentration goes hand-in-hand with your advancing consciousness.

You recognize your true nature. KNOWING comes into you. You are completely aware of your SELF. You know all these suggestions to be true. They are your reality. (Pause)

When ready, awaken your self or your client from hypnosis and your session is complete.

"…the mysterious butterflies of the soul, the beating of whose wings may someday clarify the secret of mental life."

—**Santiago Ramon y Cajal**

Chapter Fifteen
WHAT YOUR DREAMS HAVE TO SAY

Bushmen of the Kalahari and Australian Aborigines believe that human experience is only God dreaming them. Other indigenous ones receive prophecy in dreams that shape the future. For the industrialized, the idea that we are dreamed up by a higher power is challenging. Do you grasp (or not grasp) the idea that you dream your reality?

Ancient Greeks and Romans visited dream temples where they searched their dreams for massages from the gods. Artemidourus, a Greek philosopher, said: *"Dreams hold the future, analyze, and they prophesize."*

Many inventors have had their inspirations while snoozing. Chemist August Kekule discovered the structure of the benzene molecule in a dream. He wrote: *"One night I turned my chair to the fire and sank into a doze. I then dreamed of atoms swirling and settling into six circling 'snakelike' patterns. One of the serpents caught his own tail and the ring thus formed whirled exasperatedly before my eyes. I awoke as if by lightening and spent the rest of the night working out logical consequences of the hypothesis."*

Before going to sleep, ask your subconscious to offer a solution to something you want to explore or resolve. If you've lost or forgotten something you want to retrieve say: "When I awaken, I will remember. It will come back to me." The Mexican Indians train children to relieve worry by telling their trouble to little yarn wrapped dolls. Then they put the dolls under their pillow and sleep. When they awaken, the dolls have solved the problems.

When a dream reveals itself to you, listen to your inner symbolism and "interview" your inner voices and guides. With dreams, you can explore altered states like out of body experiences, past lives and spiritual encounters. These insights enhance your present day experiences and let you re-member that you are body, mind and spirit; also conscious, subconscious and superconscious.

KNOWING DREAMS

Knowing dreams is a Cosmic Consciousness insight and a source of profound creative inspiration. An ancient sutra tells it this way: *"Meditate on KNOWING what comes during sleep and many things will be uncovered within your being. To do this, move into sleep with awareness."*

Sleep and dreams have always been associated together. Most commonly, people simply fall into sleep, as if it is a sort of absence. It is not. Sleep has its own presence. Sleep exists as a state of mind, just as waking exists as a state of mind. Sleep is not just rest from waking, it is a different kind of activity, hence dreams.

Dreaming is a tremendous activity that takes you deeper into your being than thinking. When you go to sleep, the conscious part of your mind takes a rest while your subconscious and superconscious, who needs no rest, is vitally active. The superconscious is vast, omnipotent, omnipresent and omniscient. It is infinite.

The pathway to Cosmic Consciousness leads you to your superconscious mind. During sleep, you tap, via the subconscious, your inner reservoir of wisdom.

You've been trained to identify with the conscious mind while awake. It is important to identify with the subconscious during sleep. This moves you to sleep with awareness.

When you read this book you are on a conscious level; when you are aware of what is written on these pages, you are on a subconscious level. Notice the distinction. It takes practice to move into sleep with awareness and it is well worth it, as sleeping with awareness brings in much wisdom.

When you sleep with awareness, you enter the tremendous realm of creative dreams. You will note the gap that occurs as the conscious phase of mind fades into the sub and super conscious phase of mind. In that gap between the two, you will catch a glimpse of your life in all time and space. As you observe yourself drop into sleep, watch your dreams, and you will find five types of dreams occur:

TYPES OF DREAMS
Mind Scraps

The first type of dream throws off trivia gathered during the day so the mind cleanses itself. This type of dream is very common and has scant value. Bypass such dreams.

Into-Wishin'

The second type of dream is a form of wish fulfillment. You have many natural needs which need fulfillment. Be attentive to this type of dream, as it tells you what your real needs are. Your real needs are recognized by your subconscious. Real needs are not conjured by your conscious mind. Dream wishes place your behavior under your direct control.

Cosmo Topper

The third type of dream comes from your superconscious and provides guidance for your life. In this kind of dream, you recognize your spiritual nature, divinity and oneness with the Cosmos. It is dreams of Cosmic Consciousness nature. Have you ever had a profoundly moving dream? This is your superconscious mind speaking to you.

Regressions Past

The fourth type of dream is of past lifetimes. These bring in vistas from ages past. They are important, as they remind you of your immortality. Through regressive dreams, your entire understanding of existence takes on more meaning. Such dreams alter or gestalt your nature. You become aware of past mistakes and avoid repeating them. You glean wisdom from the past.

FUTURE PROGRESSIONS

The fifth type of dreams goes forward into the future, with ESP, premonition, and prognostication. Such dreams come when you are exceedingly perceptive or need a revelation to guide you.

Sutra says: *"Meditate on knowledge that comes in during sleep."* If you do, you'll have many inventive and creative breakthroughs during dreams. The more you advance in Cosmic Consciousness, the more significant your dreams.

Watching your dreams while you sleep is the secret. Learn to keep your mind alert even while the body sleeps. Your body needs sleep to renew physical vitality; mind does not.

Most prefer to go unconscious while they sleep; They escape. A Mastermind considers unconscious sleep a decided waste of a great opportunity. For them, sleep allows for the discovery of deep knowledge.

Keep your mind awake while your body sleeps and you'll advance your consciousness and become more awake while you are awake.

The easiest way to learn conscious dreaming is to become more conscious of your bodily activity while awake. This full mindfulness will then penetrate your sleep.

Start by becoming consciously aware of all that you do. Most people are only slightly aware while awake; leaving their wakeful self with little energy. You have to bring enough energy to the sleep mode so that when your conscious mind goes to sleep, awareness continues on its own. Then, you fall asleep with awareness.

Do all that you do with awareness. Considering whatever you do as practice for your inner training of mindfulness. The activity becomes secondary, and awareness, through the activity becomes primary. At night, when you go to sleep, that awareness continues while your body sleeps. During sleep, peer deep into your being and discover (uncover) what is there. Fall asleep with awareness, and as this sutra says, MEDITATE ON THE KNOWLEDGE THAT SLEEP BRINGS.

"*The development of science and of creative
activities of spirit in general requires still another
kind of freedom, which may be characterized as inward
freedom…independence of thought from restrictions
of authoritarian, social prejudices…routine and habit.*"

-Albert Einstein

Chapter Sixteen
THE ART OF MEDITATION

Meditation is a fine pathway to Cosmic Consciousness. Meditation embraces the peace and bliss that passeth all understanding. Meditation moves thoughts from the mind to the heart. Over five thousand years ago, in the sacred Vigyana Bhairvana Tantra, Shiva wrote one hundred and twelve techniques for meditation.

In Sanskrit:

Vigyana means consciousness.

Bhairvana means divine love.

Tantra means to bring consciousness to divine love.

"Be conscious of divine love to bring consciousness to divine love."

In modern times, meditation has gained popularity. We call it contemplation, concentration, visualization, prayer, going inside, turning our attention inward and ultra deep hypnosis. No matter what it's called, people in the East and West meditate. This is good.

But, in some ways, the truth is missed. Meditation is not something you do at certain times, in certain places and in certain positions. Meditation is a way of living every moment fully, to the hilt, in the here and now. Profound meditation lets you pursue your life from the heightened perspective of Cosmic Consciousness.

Meditation advances your awareness of your SELF.

The Zen Way demonstrates reality rather than talks about it. So, let's demonstrate an effective method that you can use to meditate all the time.

It is based in breathing. That's handy as you are always breathing.

Ask yourself an honest question: "Have you been aware of your breathing while you were reading this book?" As you think about it, you become aware. Five minutes from now will you be unaware again? Most likely.

BREATH MEDITATION

This method of meditation makes you very much aware. In the Orient, breath is called: "The bridge to the Universe." Breath is the sustainer of life in the physical body. Shiva presents breathing as his very first technique of meditation. Of this technique, his sutra says: *"Radiant One, this experience dawns between two breaths."*

Breathe in and consciously note your breath coming into your body. Feel the breath hit the nostrils and enter the passages of your lungs. Feel it as completely as you can. At the point just before you exhale, observe. Just for a moment, there is no breathing.

Then, exhale the breath and consciously experience air passing out of your body. Be aware of the breathless point after you do that.

Just before you again inhale, there is no breathing. Become aware of this point before you inhale the next breath. Become keenly aware of this moment. When the breath comes in, it is birth to the body, and when the breath goes out, it is death to the body. And so, your breathing continues automatically, bringing both life and death to the body. Between each in and each out breath, there is a gap, a small death. To become aware of this gap is to experience the eternal element, the rebirth and death which is YOU.

Occasionally you know that you are breathing, but have you ever been aware of the gaps between the breathing? Try it. Experience it. Note the gaps.

Move in with the breath. Then move out with the breath. Feel yourself breathing consciously in and out, in and out, in and out.

Do not go ahead of the breath or behind the breath. Just be with the breath precisely. Be in the moment of your breath. Then, experience the gaps between the breaths. This meditation of breath consciousness let's you stand in a realm between life and death.

This technique was most favored by Buddha. It has been used for centuries by millions in Tibet, China, Japan, Burma and India.

How can such a simple thing like awareness of the gaps in your breath going in and out of your body advance consciousness? Right there is the secret. It makes you aware of a very basic process of which most are unaware. Think of it, are you aware of breathing? When you remember to be continuously aware of your breath, and the gaps between the breaths, you are "being here now" or what Shiva calls a state of: *"Beneficence," "Illumination," "Enlighten-ment" or "Cosmic Consciousness."* Zen Masters call this state, "Zazen."

As mind follows breath into the inner world and out of the outer world, you discover one world. Mind becomes pure and calm. Air in and out is like a swinging door that moves us with no mind, no body; a swinging door.

The more you practice the art of Breath Meditation, the better you use it.

LISTENING MEDITATION

"The wireless telegraph is easy to understand. The ordinary telegraph is like a long cat. You pull the tail in New York and it meows in Los Angeles. The wireless is the same without the cat."

–Albert Einstein

Another technique to reach Cosmic Consciousness is listening.

Listen to the birds, breezes, music, traffic and people talking. Just listen and let your ears become the door that allows great peace.

Always meditate for nothing at all; WITH NO PURPOSE. It brings in the Realization that "I AM I."

When you can instinctively understand yourself as "I AM I," you get closer to achieving the fifth level. Satori is close by. What a joy the SEARCH brings to you. How wonderful it is to KNOW THY SELF.

HYPNOTIC HELPER:
Play the *Serenity Resonance Sound* audio tape. This Alpha Theta sound tape brings in heightened awareness. It was created by Ormond McGill and sound researcher, Joseph Worrell.

PART FOUR
ACHIEVEMENTS
FROM YOUR SEARCH

"The pursuit of truth and beauty is a sphere of activity in which we are permitted to remain children all out lives."

-Albert Einstein

"In the spiritual world, past, present and future is a quivering moment ceaselessly moving on."

-Shelley Stockwell

Chapter Seventeen
FROM PERCEPTION
TO SUPERPERCEPTION

Intuition is the language created by your mind, through which you gain direct insight. How do you achieve such cosmic insight?

First, understand that knowledge is information given you from an outside source. Information you take in from outside yourself, you call "learning." Wisdom is information you take from inside yourself and that is called, "direct perception." Information from Cosmic Consciousness and direct perception frequently comes in "flashes" of insight, often in an instant. One moment it is not there, and the next, it is.

Cosmic Conscious Insight advances your mind from perception to Superperception. The Eastern sutra expresses it well. Sutra is a Sanskrit term meaning thread; a thread that unravels to reveal truth. Have fun unraveling Patanjali's thread: *"When the activity of the mind is under control, the mind becomes like pure crystal, reflecting equally, without distortion: the perceiver, the perception and the perceived."*

To understand this sutra, peek deeply into the nature of your mind.

Your mind is not a thing, but an event. A thing has substance and an event is a process. An event is like a wave. The wave is just the event between the heavens, earth, wind and the sea. Your mind is like the wave upon the sea. It has no substance and can disappear without leaving a trace. Your mind leaves no footprints behind.

Fast moving continuous thoughts give you an illusion that something tangible called mind exists. You think; there is a mind. But, mind does not really exist; only your thoughts do. Embrace this notion that mind doesn't exist and thoughts do, and a new perception comes to you. Your thoughts, like passing clouds constantly change shape as they move across the sky. YOU are the sky. Immediately you'll perceive that you are not directly involved in your thoughts. Thoughts pass through you like wind passes through a tree. Thoughts pass because, you are in reality, vast emptiness. Nothing exists to prevent thoughts passing.

YOU are infinite sky, across which cloud-like thoughts simply come and go. Most thoughts are not original with you at all. They come from the outside. Sometimes they rest in you, that's all. What can you do about thoughts? Nothing need be done; just like a cloud resting on top of a hill; they will move on their own.

If you simply observe thoughts without getting involved, you attain control. Actually, the word "control" is not accurate. For in truth, there is nobody in control and there is nobody to be controlled. It just may help you consider that your mind is under the control of you the master, rather than visa versa.

Recognize that thoughts do not originate in you and then your thoughts then lose power over you. Thoughts cannot do anything to you; they simply come and go. You remain untouched, like a lotus flower amidst rainfall; drops of water fall on the petals and slip off. The lotus remains untouched. In the East, the lotus is a significant symbol. It represents three dimensions of consciousness:

The root, is the part of you beneath your awareness.

The lily pad represents your physical nature on earth.

The blossom reaches skyward to touch other dimensions of godliness. "Be like a lotus and remain like a lotus." Let thoughts slide away as you remain balanced.

There are a few more things about your mind that is well for you to understand.

Mind is a disturbance of consciousness, just like ocean waves disturb the ocean. Something foreign enters to produce a storm or ripple on the surface of the ocean. The wind thoughts cause a storm or ripple on the surface of your consciousness. But, the storm is only on the surface and does not disturb the depths at all. Move inward to your depths, and the surface storm on the surface is bypassed. At your center of being, all is calm and serene. Alter your perception and suddenly, you recognize that while your surface may seem disturbed, you are not disturbed. Use this awareness with pain. Rise above thoughts of pain and you are not disturbed.

In 865 BC, The Hindu sage, the "Father of Yoga," the Einstein of the Masters, Patanjali, said: *"When you look (perceive) from your center, you relax and are not worried. Storms on the surface will pass. And even a storm can be enjoyed. A storm has beauty and adventure when viewed from the safety of your center. Trouble comes when you get caught up in the storm on your surface. Worry is like riding a small boat on the surface of the ocean when the winds whip up a storm. You are worried; scared to death. It seems you are in danger and that at any moment the storm can destroy you. What can you do with your small boat? How can you keep control? If you fight the waves, you will be defeated. If you accept the waves and let your boat ride with them you will be safe."*

That's what Lao Tsu's: *"Flow with the Tsu"* means. And Tilopa's: *"Be loose and natural in relation to existence."* And what our: "Go with the flow and don't sweat the small stuff" (and it's all about small stuff) means.

Waves are there, the storm is there, but you simply allow it to be. You simply allow yourself to ride with the waves and not struggle against them. Then tremendous happiness happens. You come to know that even the storm can be enjoyed; this is CENTERING.

Centering is consciousness in control of mind. You don't try to control the mind; you simply place yourself in your center (consciousness) and you are in control without trying. Trying to control the mind is nothing but a part of the mind trying to control another part of the mind. Understanding this saves you from becoming neurotic.

Witnessing life gives you a new perspective. You let the storm on the surface simply be a source of energy. It provides strength and there is nothing to worry about. The storms of life serve to make you stronger. Mind and thoughts are part of the way of existence and existence is perfect. Nothing is wrong with your mind and nothing is wrong with your thoughts. "Problems" are on the surface with partial perception. Whole perception is needed, and that is possible only from your center. From the center you can look in all directions and view the whole of your being inside and out. It is vast. That is what is meant by Superperception and inner harmony.

Personality, Memory, and Mind

"A mediocre mind cannot understand it when one does not thoughtlessly submit to hereditary prejudices, but honestly and courageously uses his intelligence."

–Albert Einstein

The word "personality" comes from a Latin root: *persona;* the mask an actor used in ancient Roman dramas to hide their face. Your personality is not the real you. Personality is simply a false face you show to others. Through many lives and experiences, you create many personalities. You may have used them so much that your original face seems lost. Most folks forget what their original face is like. If you would like to see your original face, drop all personalities. If you cling to them, you see only a mask. To drop personalities, just be natural. Drop your old personalities as dust gathered during your long journey. You are so much more than this historical hysterical illusion.

The past is memory and memory is dust. Everybody gathers his or her own dust. It is the way existence operates, but there is no need to identify with the dust. Shake it off and be who you are. If you become one with dust, you'll be in trouble because you are not the dust, you are Consciousness.

Omar Khayam says: *"Dust unto dust."* When a man dies, what happens? If you are just dust, then everything will return to the dust and nothing will be left behind. But, you are not just dust; there is something inside you beneath the dust. That something is your consciousness; your awareness. Superperception lets you recognize this divine heritage.

Your mind is the dust that collects on your consciousness. Nature's way to clean such dust is simply to move like a snake out of your old skin and not look back. As Tilopa says: *"Just be loose from beyond the mind, which is the position of no-mind."*

Don't worry, you won't lose your mind. But, your thoughts will lose their influence. When your cooperation is gone, thoughts simply stop affecting you. They are still there, but you now witness them from your new position of Superperception. It is a tremendous difference.

Thoughts come only when you invite them to come. They never

come by themselves. Sometimes you may think: "I never invited this thought." But, in some way, maybe unconsciously, you must have invited it; otherwise it would not have come. Sometimes thoughts become so "conditioned" that even when you do not deliberately invite them, they knock on your door to be invited in. Old habits are like that. If you don't cooperate, they will stop. When thoughts stop coming on their own, this is control. It is not that you control thoughts, you simply perceive them from your center of being. Then, thoughts control themselves.

Look upon your mind as memory that has accumulated experiences of the past. Your mind remembers all that you have done, all that you have thought, all that you have desired, all that you dreamed…everything. You must rise above these memories to be able to control your mind.

How do you rid yourself of disturbing memory? Become a witness to them. Remember, memory represents what has happened to you. It is a happening you were involved in, but it is not YOU.

You have a name to identify yourself. Of course, somebody gave you that name. It has utility, but the name is not YOU.

You have a form, but the form is not YOU. The form is just the body YOU have chosen to be in. Your parents gave you the seeds of your body package. It is a gift, but it is not YOU. The secret that rids you of memory is to watch and discriminate constantly. Keep on discriminating, and a moment will come when you have eliminated everything that you are not. Suddenly, in that state, you encounter your True Being. Rise above identities that are not YOU: family, your body, your mind, your work. When everything that is not really YOU has been neutralized, your BEING surfaces. Then you encounter your SELF, and that encounter is the control of mind.

Usually, we think of control being an outside phenomenon with something or someone controlling you. This control is the inside YOU controlling the outside superficial you.

Patanjali's sutra transforms normal perception to Superperception: *When the activity of the mind is under control, the mind becomes like pure crystal, reflecting equally without distortion; the perceiver, the perception and the perceived.*

Let's continue unraveling this sutra thread…

When the activity of the mind is under control by your SELF, you are at your center. You eliminate from your perception all that you have become identified with: your form, your name, your personality, and even your mind. Only things, which cannot be eliminated, remain. This is precisely what the Upanishads, meant by: *"I am not this; not that."*

The moment comes when only the "witness" remains, and the "witness" cannot be denied, for it is the Center of Your Being. You no longer are identified with your body. Only your inner SELF is fact. Then your mind becomes quiet and under control. When you are quiet inside, you cause your mind to be quiet outside.

If you think you can force your mind to be silent on the outside, and by so doing that you will become silent on the inside, you show that you do not understand the science of silence. The secret is when you become silent inside, the outside will overflow with magnificent silence. The periphery of yourself follows the center of your SELF; the reverse is impossible. Always remember that the whole search for enlightenment is from the inside towards the outside and not vice versa. When that happens, then you are in control of your mind, and when the mind is under control, the mind becomes like pure crystal.

It is a Cosmic Consciousness achievement.

Become silent inside yourself and you use your mind in a superb manner. The mind is there just as it always has been. When silent inside, thoughts come and go. When viewed from your silent center, you are neither for nor against thoughts, you are indifferent or positively neutral. You cannot learn this, you have to feel it. When you do, you witness your mind and the way it operates and you remain untouched by it. You become master of your mind and use it superbly to its full capacities. All confusion from your perception is removed. Your mind, free of confusion, is open to Superperception.

Nobody brings order to their mind by *trying* to bring order to it. Attempting to bring order creates more confusion. If you simply become silent inside and wait; then observe with indifference, as things settle themselves. This invariably happens, for it is a fundamental law of existence that things cannot remain unsettled for long. An unsettled state is unnatural. A settled state is natural. Just watch, wait and be indifferent and the settlement will come on its own. *"Nothing need to be done"* is a direct quotation from Buddha.

Nature loves order. Chaos is a temporary state. Always, we

return to homeostasis or balance. Simply watch any confusion and mind will settle by itself. When the mind settles, its activity comes under control and the mind becomes like pure crystal. Nothing causes the mind to settle more rapidly than the neutrality of being neither for, nor against.

Buddha calls it *upeksha,* which means *absolute and total indifference.* You sit by the flowing river as things settle in the swirling waters and suddenly the stream is crystal clear.

When your mind becomes perfectly clear, it functions like a three-dimensional mirror. The objective outside world reflects in it, the subjective inside world reflects in it, and the relationship between the two is reflected...without distortion. This is the phenomenon of Superperception.

*"As far as the laws of mathematics refer
to reality, they are not certain, and as far as they
are certain, they do not refer to reality."*

-Albert Einstein

Chapter Eighteen
WONDER FULL DIRECT PERCEPTION

Direct perception is pure, unblemished and immediate. Have you ever played the old game of gossip where you whisper a message, one by one around the circle of people? In the end, the original message is distorted. That's how indirect information turns out.

Knowledge is indirect. With knowledge, a messenger carried information to you. The messenger distorts the message. Ancient Tibetan teachings say of direct perception: *"An object is experienced in its full perspective, directly, without the use of the senses. The perception gained in this way transcends all normal perception both in extent and intensity."*

The Yogic term Nirvikalpa Samadhi means that you perceive and conceive truth immediately. Wonderfully matter-of-fact it says: *"The perception gained in Nirvikalpa Samadhi transcends all normal perceptions, both in extent and intensity."*

Knowledge is Unreliable

"Put your hand on a hot stove for a minute and it seems like an hour. Sit with a pretty girl for an hour and it seems like a minute. That's reality."

–Albert Einstein

Knowledge comes to your senses from outside yourself. Next, your senses carry it through the nervous system. Your nervous system sends it to the brain. Finally, the brain delivers it to the mind, and then mind delivers it to you (or possibly vice versa). This is an indirect detour from the source of knowledge.

When nerves bring a message to your brain, the brain decodes it. However, it has no way of checking as to whether or not the message the nerves carry is real or unreal. The brain has to depend upon the reliability of the nerves and the brain then transmits the message (just as it is received) to the mind. The mind has no way to check the brain, and simply has to believe it. The mind relays the message. This roundabout process clouds consciousness with distorted information.

The mechanism of knowledge is difficult to check. Because you perceive it though your body.

Consciousness is not rooted in the body; the body is just housing. Just as you can go in and out of your house, so consciousness can go in and out of your body. In other words, consciousness bypasses the whole body mechanism and looks at things directly. Such "looking," is the perception of wisdom.

NIRVIKALPA SAMADHI

"It is only to the individual that a soul is given."

–Albert Einstein

In Nirvikalpa Samadhi, when death occurs, thoughts cease. Thought is the connection between mind and consciousness. Without thought, you don't have mind, and when you don't have mind, the connection with the brain and nervous system is broken. Then your consciousness flows in and out. But, you don't have to keel over to have this experience.

"In the state of Nirvikalpa Samadhi, all doors are opened and your consciousness is free to perceive directly."

You perceive directly and immediately when there is no "messengers" between you and the source of wisdom.

You cannot imagine direct perception, because it is not part of imagination. When you look at a flower through the eyes of Cosmic Consciousness, you see the flower as it really is. Not only do you perceive the flower, but through the flower you see the whole of existence, for the flower is part of the whole. In a leaf dancing in the wind, the WHOLE dances. In the smile on the face of a human being, GOD smiles.

Free yourself from the prison of your senses and your entire perception changes and advances. Form melts into formless, and then into a vast ocean of beauty.

Direct perception is vastly different from normal perception. In direct perception, each is conscious to the degree it is, the entire universe is seen as one vast eternal consciousness, and everything in it is part of the whole and whole is unto itself.

You experience a part of the whole, and the whole as ONE.

In the state of Nirvikalpa Samadhi, an object is experienced in its full perspective, because in this state, knowledge is gained directly without the use of the senses. Bypass your senses and your perception is unlimited. Relying on your senses is like looking through a keyhole at the sky. The keyhole gives its own frame to the sky and distorts everything. The sky will not be bigger than the keyhole. How can your perspective be bigger than your hand through which you touch? How can a sound be deeper than your ears through which you hear? Your senses are "keyholes." Through them, you look at reality. Reality, as you perceive it through your senses, is distorted. When you perceive directly, you jump out of your limitations of reality, into THE INFINITE! The beginning and end is not there. There are no boundaries in existence. All limitations belong to your senses.

RELEASE LIMITS

"Any thinking physicist must come to the conclusion that time and space are illusions."

-Albert Einstein

Existence itself is infinite.

Before the vast universe, your ego simply becomes irrelevant. What you thought was YOU disappears and the real YOU remains. Cosmic Consciousness makes your perspective so full that ego disappears.

Existence IS vastness. This is the concept of THE VOID.

When you advance to direct perception, you step out of the mechanism of limits. You directly intuit reality. In full perspective, an object is experienced as it really is: vastness.

The object joins infinity. It cannot exist without infinity. So, it is with YOU.

When you bypass limits, telepathy is the natural avenue of communication. Your mind enjoys clairvoyance, PSI (physical/psychic intuitive manifestations) and other extra perception powers.

DIRECT PERCEPTION

With full perception, everything is revealed. Whatever you want to do immediately happens (instant manifestation). Action is not needed. That is what Lao Tzu means when he says: *"The sage lives in inactivity and everything happens."* Miracles happen when you come out of your body. The actual miracle was never done. This is the basic quality of a miracle…it is never DONE…it HAPPENS. A miracle is not a demonstration; it is a transformation of beingness.

When Buddha moves, it is said that many things happen invisibly. Few understand what is happening because these things belong to an unknown world. You don't have language or concept for it and, you cannot see it unless it happens to you. When your mind advances to its no-mind state, miracles happen. That is the meaning of full perspective. When consciousness faces consciousness, Nirvikalpa Samadhi is achieved.

What happens when a mirror faces another mirror? One mirror mirrors another mirror ad-infinitum; mirrors reflecting each other millions of times.

WHEN CONSCIOUSNESS FACES CONSCIOUSNESS, THE WHOLE UNIVERSE BECOMES LIKE MILLIONS OF MIRRORS AND YOU ARE ALSO A MIRROR.

"The perception gained in Nirvikalpa Samadhi transcends all normal perceptions, both in extent and intensity."

The words "extent" and "intensity" are very meaningful. When you see the world through the senses, plus the brain and the mind, the world is not seen with the luminosity that is actually there. Normal perception is not at full perception. With full perception, an entirely new brilliant world is there.

Those who take mind-influencing drugs, like LSD, report seeing a world remarkably altered; often luminescent and beautiful. They may think that the world appears glorious because of the drug. Not so. All the drug has done is shock the senses and stimulate the brain in such a way that for a limited time, the eyes take a peek at the world as it really is. Drugs are a foolish way to do this, for the drug shocks your awareness only for a few hours and then is gone. Then, the world seems duller to the senses than even before. To attain that state again through drugs requires more drugs. Humans become immune to the drug and before long all its effectiveness is

---

gone. The effects of LSD or other drugs are as nothing.

In the book, *The Holographic Mind*, a story is told about LSD guru, Harvard psychologist Richard Alpert, who in 1966 observed the reactions of LSD on holy men. One 60 plus-year-old holy man from the Himalayas was offered 50-75 micrograms of LSD (considered a small dosage). The man insisted on taking a whopping 950 micrograms.

Aghast, Alpert expected a dramatic reaction. Yet, the fellow behaved normally all day long. Except for a twinkling glance now and then in Alpert's direction, the LSD apparently affected him not.

Alpert was so astounded by this man, that he gave up LSD, changed his name to Ram Dass and converted to mysticism. *"Often, we only know we've been in a certain place when we pass beyond it,"* he said.

A single moment of enlightenment lets you know a world millions of times more glorious than any glimpse drugs give you. In Nirvikalpa Samadhi, you see reality directly with your consciousness. Your perception is clear. You look at the whole shebang of vast existence. Now, there is no barrier, your vision is infinite.

This is intense. Flowers will be recognized as persons, trees as friends and rocks as sleeping souls.

You will then understand what Tennyson wrote: *"If I could understand a flower, a small flower in its totality, I would have understood it all."* If you can understand the part, you can then understand the whole, because the part is the whole.

Ordinary mathematics says that the part can never be bigger than the whole. This is a simple maxim of mathematics. Einstein, did not agree with this.

When you come from beyond your mind and senses, a higher mathematics comes clear as crystal. The maxim of this higher mathematics is:

The part is always the whole; the part is never smaller that the whole. Sometimes, the part seems ever bigger than the whole.

The higher mathematics of the universe is quite beyond the comprehension of the normal mind, but consciousness recognizes it immediately. When viewed, via direct perception, relativity is how things are.

A pebble is a very small part of the whole. However, look at it with direct consciousness and suddenly the pebble becomes the whole. In reality, there is only the oneness where no part is apart or separate. In fact, the part depends on the whole and the whole depends on the part for its existence.

If you cut a hologram in a thousand pieces, each piece contains within it the entire hologram. Think of the pebble or yourself as a hologram.

The mystic Eckhart expresses this truth so nicely: *"I depend on you God, but you equally depend on me. If I were not here, who would worship and who would pray? You would miss me."*

Eckhart is not expressing ego in this simple fact. He tells the truth that everything exists together: the worshipper and the worshipped exist together; the lover and the beloved exist together. One cannot exist without the other. Again, this is the essence of existence...everything exists together.

Cosmic Consciousness is identified with many names.

Cosmic Consciousness belongs to all races, creeds, social and educational stratas. Sometimes knowledge stands in the way of KNOWING. When will your Cosmic Consciousness be in full flower?

Ultimately it comes to everyone.

A new world opens to you when you KNOW that the Creator and Creation are ONE; THE ALL IN ALL; THE TOTALITY. When this understanding is clear as crystal, YOU KNOW IT HAS BEEN A DARN SUCCESSFUL SEARCH.

*"To know that what is impenetrable to us
really exists, manifesting itself as the highest
wisdom and the most radiant beauty which our
dull faculties can comprehend only in their
primitive forms, this knowledge, this feeling
is the CENTER OF TRUE EXPERIENCE."*

-Albert Einstein

Chapter Nineteen
YOUR GLORIOUS IMMORTALITY

When you achieve Cosmic Consciousness, you accept your immortality. You know that you have lived many LIFE TIMES.

The cycle of the formless into form and form into formless is called reincarnation. Whether you believe or don't believe in reincarnation is irrelevant. In the Universe, everything is patterned on birth, death and rebirth. The cells in your body die and are replaced. Winter turns to spring.

Even the stars follow this pattern. A star is born; it exists for eons of time and finally dies to become a "black hole" in space. More eons pass and its energy is renewed and a new star is born.

Every living person is immortal. When you first arrived here in this lifetime, you remembered where you came from and where you are going. Later, veils of illusion clouded these memories. As you lift these veils, you re-embrace your cosmic awareness.

We have all died many deaths and enjoyed many births. What we call birth is merely the reverse side of death. Like a door marked "entrance" on the outside (your physical body) and "exit" (the transition from your body at the time called "death") on the inside. Life and death are the flip side of the same coin.

Some have no conscious memory of their many births and deaths. Few remember their recent birth and yet no one doubts they were born. The field of our human perception is extremely limited. There are objects we cannot see, sounds we cannot hear, odors we cannot smell, tastes we cannot taste and feelings we cannot feel. But, we have proof that with our obvious physical limitations, they exist.

Many years ago evolution was a theory believed in by few. Today, the majority accepts it. Evolution is the evolvement of the physical body, while reincarnation is the evolvement of the soul. Body after body, life experience after life experience, transforms and evolves your soul's growth.

In the English translation of the Bible, Christ says: *"Except that a man be born again, he cannot enter the Kingdom of God."* Christian doctrine has interpreted "born again" as meaning a spiritual rebirth. The original Hebrew text however, has it written as: *"Except that a man be born again and again, he cannot enter into the Kingdom of Heaven."* In the Koran, it is written: *"God generates beings and then sends them back over and over again until they return to Him."*

Voltaire wrote: *"After all, it is no more surprising to be born twice than it is to be born once. Everything in Nature is resurrection."* Niezsche states: *"Live, so that thou mayest desire to live again, that is thy duty. For, in any case, thou wilt live again!"*

How long will the process of rebirth continue for the soul? From Cosmic Consciousness comes an answer to that question: *For as long as the desire for the physical world is there, the soul reincarnates.*

Some say the process is endless. Because of nonlinear time, in four-dimensional space, there is really no before or after and therefore no cause and effect. Some say that the process is limited because we choose whether or not to come back to physical rebirth. Some say we are external and all life is our own. Reincarnation is an idea presented from our human viewpoint of linear time. But, eternity is non-linear and timeless; thus in all cases we eternally exist.

Self-Consciousness to Cosmic Consciousness brings you closer to acceptance of immortality and reincarnation.

The Upanishads say it this way: *"As a man's desire is, so is his destiny. For as his desire, so is his will, as is his deed. And, as his deed is, so is his reward, whether good or bad. For a man acts according to the desires he treasures.*

After death, he goes to the next world bearing in his mind, subtle impressions of these deeds. After reaping the harvest of his deeds, he returns again to the world of action. Thus, he who still has the desires of the Earth, continues subject to rebirth. But, he who has no earthly desires, who has discrimination, whose mind is steady and whose heart is pure and does not desire to be reborn, reaches the goal, and having reached it, is form no more, and remains amongst the hosts with God."

*"If the doors of perception were cleansed,
everything would appear as it is, infinite."*

- William Blake

Chapter Twenty
OM & THE BLUE FLAME

Your fantastic Cosmic Consciousness goes on and on, fascinating and spiraling you upwards ever-expanding into what IS.

Here is an experience that lifts you higher: The OM and THE BLUE FLAME. You can hear the sound of OM echoing within your being and see the BLUE FLAME billow within your heart. When you do, all becomes serene and joyous.

Some night when the sky is clear and the stars shine brightly, go outside and look up into the vast cosmos and become one with it.

Cup your hands over your ears and press in gently. Then, out loud with the Universe spread before your gaze, intone six times the sound of OM:

OM, OM, OM, OM, OM, OM

In India, OM is known as the God sound and the basis of all sounds. Both hear and feel it reverberate through your Being. Still gazing into the heavens, drop your hands to your sides and go silent. Then LISTEN. Now, keeping your eyes open, meditate on the inner light that the echoing sound brings to your attention. Close your eyes and find a flame...a beautiful flame of blue light burning near your heart. You will see it, for the truth is, it is always there. It has always been there. You can see the Inner Light within your body because you have developed your powers of perception with Cosmic Consciousness.

Photos of the "blue flame" have been captured on very sensitive film. Manifested on the surface of the body it is called the aura. The source of the blue flame is your Heart Center deep within your body. When your body dies, that blue light goes out of your body. Its body-energy leaves and disappears into the cosmos. Many report observing this "flame" leaving the body of a person at their moment of death.

At first, you may see only darkness, just as you do when you go from sunlight into a darkened room. If nothing seems to be there except darkness, wait! Just wait and look down into your heart. Suddenly it will happen; you'll see a blue light, a flame. When you do, concentrate on that flame.

Seeing and/or experiencing your "inner flame" produces an experience of complete bliss. It makes you feel like dancing and singing. Nothing is more musical or harmonious than the inner blue light within your heart. The more you concentrate upon it, the more you become tranquil, calm and silent. There is no darkness when your heart center is filled with light, the whole universe is seen as filled with light.

Photo by Jon Nicholas

"The collective unconscious contains the whole spiritual heritage of humankind's evolution, born anew in the brain structure of every individual."

-Carl Jung

Chapter Twenty One
THE NEVER-ENDING SEARCH

Your search has been intense. One concise suggestion says it all: You are a timeless miracle. YOU is your unique self. TIMELESS is recognition of your immortality. And MIRACLE expresses the totality of your being: It is a miracle that you exist.

How will you know when your search for Cosmic Consciousness has been successful? It is impossible for you not to know, for you will find yourself. You will become aware of your intimate relationship with Existence.

In perfect harmony with the Universe every thing seems so simple and self-operating. You instantly manifest all that you request. You will wonder how you ever missed such clarity.

Filled with bliss and utter happiness, the flame in your heart burns so brightly, your aura radiates warmth to all. You are like a cozy hearth others gather around on a cold winter's night.

This book is nearly finished. Its purpose was to help you move along the path in your SEARCH FOR COSMIC CONSCIOUSNESS. There is no going back.

Cosmic Consciousness never stops, for its unfoldment of Consciousness is Infinite. It is like eating potato chips...one bite and you want more.

What a joy! Your consciousness, ever increasing, and ever more wonderful and dazzling, becomes the Universe in which you exist.

You understand THE GREAT SPELL given humankind in the ancient Hindu Vedas: *"Therefore, the only thing worth knowing is the Prajnaparamita or great spell. This is the spell of great knowledge. The utmost spell. The unequaled spell. Gone altogether beyond. Oh, what an awakening. All hail! This completes the heart of perfect wisdom."*

This ancient sutra also explains the sign posts for advanced consciousness in the FOUR "GONES:"

1. GONE from Unconscious Consciousness
2. GONE from Simple Consciousness
3. GONE BEYOND from Self-Consciousness
4. GONE ALTOGETHER BEYOND into the realm of Cosmic Consciousness

Your complete heart of perfect wisdom knows a never-ending, ever-expanding search for greater and even greater Consciousness.

What amazing adventures lie ahead for you and us all as our wisdom advances upwards into cosmic infinity.

This is what Einstein was searching for just prior to his transition: The Grand Unified Field Theory.

The more your consciousness advances, the more you are aware of the infinite things in the universe. IT IS A NEVER ENDING SEARCH.

One thing is certain, you will never get bored. Your ever increasing wonder reminds you of Einstein when he said: *"The more I come to know, the more I realize how little I actually know and so I continue my search..."*

*How did you like the book, Master Genius? It was dedicated
to you, you know. Did we manage to get over a few ideas?*

A kindly voice from amongst the stars replies…

Guru (to hot dog vendor): *"Make me one with everything."*

Hot dog Vendor (to guru): *"Can you help me with change?"*

Guru (to hot dog vendor): *"Change comes from within."*

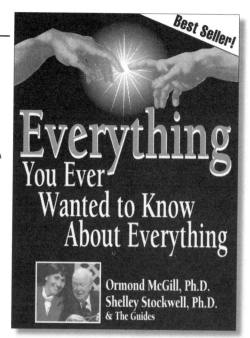

EVERYTHING YOU EVER WANTED TO KNOW ABOUT EVERYTHING

by Ormond McGill, Ph.D.
Shelley Stockwell, Ph.D.
and The Guides

Use this profound little book as a manual for your most precious possession - your life. It is filled with philosophical insights, gems for quantum leaps in your personal fulfillment and spiritual growth. Release yourself from fears and confusion, and walk your life purpose!

Everything you ever wanted to know about...

★ God	★ Wisdom	★ Joy
★ Existence	★ Money	★ Consciousness
★ Death	★ Love & Sex	★ Everything!

"Perfume for the soul."

"... a timeless bible for the new millennium."

"Each insight spread through me like rainbow ink, and I remember that I am the gold at that rainbow's end."

Audio/Book On Tape - 60 minutes
$10.00
Everything You Ever Wanted To Know About Everything &
Ten Giant Steps to Super Consciousness
ISBN #0-912559-44-6

Book
$14.95
245 pages
ISBN #0-912559-29-2

Order forms on last pages

DENIAL IS NOT A RIVER IN EGYPT

Stockwell's Hypnosis System to Life's Promised Land

by Shelley Stockwell, Ph.D.

Psst! The secret is out. Learn Hypnotherapist Stockwell's secrets that transforms denial, depression, addiction and compulsion into ecstacy, self love & joy.

Learn:

★ Ancient Secrets, Modern Wisdom

★ How to Bust Crazy Habits

★ How to Rewrite Your Life Script for Success!

★ Step-By-Step Instructions that Get Results

"Your book could help a lot of people."

– Bernie Siegel, *"Love, Medicine & Miracles"*

"I very much enjoyed what you wrote."

– Leo Buscalia, *"Living, Loving & Learning"*

Related Audio Tapes: @ $10
Lose Weight
No More Sugar Junkie
No More Alcohol
Peace and Calm
Quit Smoking
Yes, I Can

$24.95
Book - 500 pages
ISBN # 0-912559-43-8

Order forms on last pages

BOOK

HYPNOSIS
How To Put A Smile On Your Face, And $ In Your Pocket

by Shelley Stockwell, Ph.D.

After 22 years as a Hypnotherapist, Stockwell shares what hypnosis is and how to use it as a powerful tool for yourself, your family, friends, or as a career. Teaches you to tap the power of your mind to make your dreams a reality!

Learn:

★ The 10 Secrets of the Mind

★ How to be a Money Magnet

★ 42 Personal Affirmations That Bring Happiness

★ The 30 Second Stockwell Zap

★ Hypnosis Scripts

"I read your book and took your class. Your strategies really work!"
> – Raleigh Pinkskey, *"A Hundred and One Ways to Promote Yourself"*

"I read your book on hypnosis from cover to cover tonight. Only one word can describe it: Superb."
> – Ormond McGill, The Dean of American Hypnosis

"The hypnosis expert."
> – *National Enquirer*

$19.95
Book – 425 pages
ISBN #0-912559-17-9

Order forms on last pages

WINNER OF THE 1999 PEN & QUILL AWARD

Order forms on last pages

AUTOMATIC WRITING & HIERO-SCRIPTING

Tap Unlimited Creativity and Guidance

by
Shelley Stockwell, Ph.D.

AS SEEN ON THE PHIL DONOHUE SHOW!

This book teaches how to write automatically, from simple phrase to painting dramatically. What it is. How it's done. Expand your awareness while having fun!

"..drop your veil of fear and let our words move upon your page. Overflow beauty, guidance and creativity. We, your guiding angels serve and love you."
– Arch Angel Michael
written through Shelley

"Anyone who can draw, write or type can automatic write and hieroscript – this book shows how!"

$9.95
Book - 112 pages
ISBN #0-912559-25-X

Order forms on last pages

SEX & OTHER TOUCHY SUBJECTS

by Shelley Stockwell, Ph.D.

This award winning poetry book tackles love, money, sex, drugs, religion, Mom, Dad, apple pie and death. Hilariously funny and profoundly sensitive. Includes free cassette offer.

"Shelley has an eerie talent for writing MY very thoughts... To enjoy this book is to truly enjoy myself." – Kris Blake, Magic Mirrors

See Everything Book on tape, 17 songs. Brilliantly arranged by Frank Unzuata and performed by Shelley Stockwell, Frank Unzuata and Betsy Cowen.

WINNER OF THE GIFT OF THE YEAR AWARD!

$14.95
Book - 340 Pages
ISBN #0-912559-12-8

Book on Tape: @ $10
ISBN #0-912559-13-6

THE SEARCH FOR COSMIC CONSCIOUSNESS
The Hypnosis Book Einstein Would Have Loved!

by Hypnotherapists:
Ormond McGill, Ph.D. and
Shelley Stockwell, Ph.D.

"A wake up call for your soul. When these thoughts walk through your mind, the door to higher consciousness opens."
– Lynn Loa, Television Producer

$19.95
Book - 168 Pages
ISBN #0-912559-52-7

Order forms on last pages

THE SECRETS OF HYPNOTIZING WOMEN

by Hypnotherapists:
Ormond McGill, Ph.D. and
Shelley Stockwell, Ph.D.

A step-by-step manual that entrances. Women love to be loved and women love hypnosis.

"The only trouble is that when the women wake up and find Ormond is not Richard Gere—wow is he in trouble."
> —Martin St. James,
> Australia's Great Hypnotist & Author

$19.95
Book - 125 pages
ISBN # 0912559-50-0

THE SECRETS OF HYPNOTIZING MEN

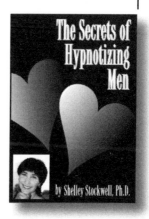

by Hypnotherapist
Shelley Stockwell, Ph.D.

Step-By-Step ways that charm him. Men can't resist being hypnotized! Includes the create a perfect mate quiz and instructions.

"Samson was a pushover."
> —Delilah

$19.95
Book - 125 pages
ISBN # 0912559-50-1

Order forms on last pages

Order forms on last pages

CHANNELING: YOU CONDUIT!

by Shelley Stockwell, Ph.D.
and Kendra, Spirit Guide

Startling spiritual secrets guide you to higher consciousness. Learn how to channel through voice, healing hands, automatic writing, intuition, visions and much more. Trance channel & hypnosis expert Stockwell shows you how!

"Hilarious, heartwarming help for channeling wisdom. Thank You."

"Funny how easily I met my guides."

$19.95
Book
ISBN #0-912559-45-4

WEDDING LOVE LETTERS
From Brides & Grooms Wildly In Love!

by Rev. Shelley Stockwell, Ph.D.

Inspirational private love letters from brides and grooms on their wedding day. The results will touch your heart, your soul, your core. Share these intimate, inspirational moments and write your own love letter.

"Intimate, funny and delightful."

$19.95
Book
ISBN #0-912559-46-2

Order forms on last pages

TRANCE-FORMATIONS

Hypnosis, Channeling & Past Life Regression

by
Shelley Stockwell, Ph.D.

Shelley Stockwell's Trance-Formations video is a riveting opportunity to explore the deepest regions of your mind through hypnosis, channeling and past life regression.

Video Tape!

Demonstrates:

- ★ Channeling
- ★ Hypnosis
- ★ Regressions
- ★ Progressions
- ★ Automatic Writing
- ★ Behavior Modification

"This video will transform the way you see yourself once and for your highest good!"

Available in Japanese too!

$19.95
Video Tape
45 minutes
ISBN #0-912559-23-3

Order forms on last pages

HYPNOTICALLY YOURS,
Ormond McGill

Shelley Stockwell
interviews Ormond
McGill, America's most
beloved hypnotist

The Dean of American Hypnosis,
Ormond McGill, Ph.D. shares his
secrets of consciousness, hypnosis
and the mind. An amazing master
teacher, Ormond has been studying
and using hypnosis for over seventy
years.

HYPNOTICALLY YOURS

Shelley Stockwell interviews
America's most beloved Hypnotist,
Ormond McGill

Video Tape!

In this candid video interview with Hypnotherapist, Shelley
Stockwell, Ph.D., McGill discusses the functions of the mind and
how you can harness its power.

Includes:
 ★ Step-by-Step Demonstrations of Hypnosis Techniques
 ★ How to Mesmerize Another
 ★ Eye Fixation
 ★ Deepening Skills
 ★ Ideomotor Impulses and Much More…

"Profound wisdom"
"Like spending the evening with fascinating friends"
"I tried several techniques and they work perfectly! Thanks."

$19.95
Video Tape
60 minutes
ISBN #0-912559-36-5

Order forms on last pages

HIGHER SELF HYPNOSIS VIDEO SERIES
3 Stunning Videos:

STOCKWELL'S SECRETS OF THE MIND

Explore the mystery and mastery of your amazing mind. *(90 minutes)*   ISBN# 0912559-48-9

McGILL'S SECRETS OF MAGIC AND STAGE HYPNOSIS

Highlights the Guardian Angel Hypnosis Show. Interviews with volunteers, and the genius of the McGill System. *(2 hours)*   ISBN# 0912559-49-7

THE SECRET LIVES OF ORMOND McGILL
A Past Life Journey

America's most famous hypnotist, 86 year old Ormond McGill, Ph.D. guided by past life therapist Shelley Stockwell Ph.D. revisits some of the world's greatest mind masters:
- James Braid
- Jean Charcot
- Franz Mesmer
- Baron Von Rochenbach

Includes a view of Atlantis as it sinks away and a private audience with the female pharaoh Hatshetsup. *(1 hour)*   ISBN# 0912559-47-0

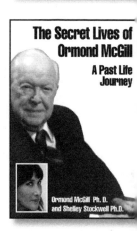

$19.95 each
$55.00 for all 3
Video Tapes

Order forms on last pages

PEACE & CALM

Created by Hypnotherapist,
Shelley Stockwell, Ph.D.

This perfect stress reducer hypnotizes
you to fall in love—with yourself!

$10.00
AudioTape
ISBN #0-912559-08-X

SLEEP, BEAUTIFUL SLEEP

Created by Hypnotherapist,
Shelley Stockwell, Ph.D.

This closed eye hypnosis tape lets you
sleep soundly and feel rested, at home
or away. Great stress buster.

$10.00
AudioTape
ISBN #0-912559-01-2

THE MONEY TAPE

By Shelley Stockwell, Ph.D.
and Joan Lessin, Ph.D.

Listen to one side as you drive in the
car, the other while you drift off to
sleep. Create energy that lets you
manifest money and opportunity.
Includes: "The Money Song" by
commodities mogul Ed Sakota.

"It Worked!"
    – Rhonda Carpenter, C.Ht..

The Money Tape

FINANCIAL FREEDOM

by Shelley Stockwell, Ph.D.
& Joan Lessin, Ph.D.

$10.00
Audio Tape - 60 min.
ISBN #0-912559-37-3

Order forms on last pages

MER•KA•BA:
Ascension to the 4th Dimension

by Shelley Stockwell, Ph.D.
Tonal Music by Wayne Perry

The famous 18 Breaths to Enlightenment! Powerful consciousness expansion for your highest good! Close your eyes and learn the ancient Egyptian initiation rite and visit other dimensions.

"A powerful and mind altering experience not to be missed!"
– Kay Risberg, Hypnotist

$10.00
AudioTape - 60 min.
ISBN #0-912559-27-6

MEET YOUR ANGEL
Closed Eye Meditation

by Shelley Stockwell, Ph.D.
Music & Vocals: Jeannie Fitzsimmons
Trumpet & Flugle Horn: Jim Hale

Cross into the world of wonder and connect with your higher self, guides and angels. Expect a miracle! Hypnotherapist and Channel Shelley Stockwell shows you how in this profound closed eye meditation.

$10.00
Audio Tape - 45 min.
ISBN #0-912559-35-7

Order forms on last pages

KUNDALINI RISING
The Ancient Rite of Enlightenment

by Ormond McGill, Ph.D.
and Shelley Stockwell, Ph.D.

Open your chakras. Written about 7000 years ago in Sanskrit, this closed eye journey opens your body and mind to light!

Kundalini Rising
The Ancient Rite of Enlightenment

Ormond McGill, Ph.D.
Shelley Stockwell, Ph.D.

"One of the most remarkable experiences of your life!"

$10.00
AudioTape - 60 min.
ISBN #0-912559-38-1

YOGA NIDRA HYPNOYOGA
The Ancient Oriental Method for Advancing to Cosmic Consciousness

by The Dean of American Hypnosis, Ormond McGill, Ph.D.

This powerful closed eye meditation opens the door to your personal enlightenment!

Yoga Nidra Hypnoyoga
The Ancient Oriental Method for Advancing to Cosmic Consciousness

By The Dean of American Hypnosis
Ormond McGill, PH.D.

"This tape changed my life."
– Shelley Stockwell, author

$10.00
Audio Tape - 60 min.
ISBN #0-912559-34-9

Order forms on last pages

THE WELLNESS TAPE
A Journey of Renewal

By Shelley Stockwell, Ph.D.
and Dr. Lilia Prado, D.O.

Hypnotherapist Shelley Stockwell and Medical Doctor Lilia Prado teach you how to feel your very best. Tap into your body's innate ability to renew, heal and revitalize. Hypnosis is not a miracle, the results just seem that way!

"I think you are angels; you helped save my life."

$10.00
AudioTape - 60 min.
ISBN #0-912559-32-2

I LOVE EXERCISE
Motivation is Fun!

By Shelley Stockwell, Ph.D.

Wow, you have a great shape! Hypno-Motivation makes exercise fun! Eliminate negative scripts and get moving again.

"Thank You Shelley!"

Audio Tape - 60 min. $10.00
ISBN #0-912559-40-3
CD $20.00
ISBN #0-912559-55-1

Order forms on last pages

AUDIO TAPES

THE VIOLET FLAME
The Most Beautiful Meditation In The World

by Ormond McGill, Ph.D.
The Dean of American Hypnosis

Enjoy the profound Hypno Yoga Journey. Close your eyes and watch a flickering candle as you drift into sacred lands.

"A tune up for the soul."
"No wonder they say Ormond McGill is a master!"

$10.00
Audio Tape - 60 min.
ISBN #0-912559-33-0

SERENITY RESONANCE SOUND

By Ormond McGill, Ph.D.
and Joseph Worrell, C.Ht..

Serenity Resonance Sound places your remarkable biocomputer brain in a receptive state to function any way you call upon it to function. These scientifically calibrated frequencies are designed to unobtrusively harmonize and evoke a peaceful mind, awake or asleep.

Audio Tape $20.00
ISBN #0-912559-53-5
CD $25.00
ISBN #0-912559-54-3

Order forms on last pages

ALL OF OUR SELF-HYPNOSIS AUDIO CASSETTES...

 EVERYTHING YOU EVER WANTED TO KNOW ABOUT EVERYTHING
10 STEPS TO SUPER CONSCIOUSNESS
Book on Tape.   ISBN #0-912559-44-6

 FLIGHT ATTENDANT WELL-BEING
A perfect attitude adjuster. Feel happy, positive. ISBN #0-912559-05-5

 GREAT GOLF
Build confidence, play focused, relaxed & improve your score!
ISBN #0-912559-20-9

 GREAT TENNIS
Improve your game, play focused & have fun! ISBN #0-912559-41-1

 I LOVE EXERCISE
Motivation is fun—gets you moving again!
ISBN #0-912559-40-3 Tape
ISBN #0-912559-55-1 CD

 KUNDALINI RISING
The ancient rite of enlightenment. A wonderful experience.
ISBN #0-912559-38-1

 LOSE WEIGHT!
Lose unwanted pounds forever, gaining energy and confidence.
ISBN #0-912559-02-0

 MAGNETIC MIND TONING
Profound Hypnotic relaxation.
ISBN #0-912559-56-X

 MEET YOUR ANGEL
Connect with your higher self, your guides and angels.
ISBN #0-912559-35-7

 MER-KA-BA: *Ascension to the 4th Dimension*
Powerful consciousness expansion for highest good.   ISBN #0-912559-27-6

 NO MORE ALCOHOL
Break free of alcohol. Feel your life again.
ISBN #0-912559-10-1

 NO MORE SUGAR JUNKIE
Bust the sugar blues. Feel alive and terrific!
ISBN #0-912559-03-9

 PEACE AND CALM
The perfect stress reducer. You need no tranquilizers.
ISBN #0-912559-08-X

 QUIT SMOKING
Save money, breathe again and feel healthy.
ISBN #0-912559-04-7

 SANDY BEACH MEDITATION
Beautiful closed-eye meditation.
ISBN #0-912559-57-8

 SERENITY RESONANCE SOUND
Alpha and theta brain waves.
ISBN #0-912559-53-5 Tape
ISBN #0-912559-54-3 CD

 SEX & OTHER TOUCHY SUBJECTS
17 Songs from Book Book on Tape.
ISBN #0-912559-13-6

 SLEEP, BEAUTIFUL SLEEP
Sleep soundly & feel rested, at home or away. Great stress buster.
ISBN #0-912559-01-2

 THE MONEY TAPE
Create energy that lets you manifest opportunity & money.
ISBN #0-912559-37-3

 THE VIOLET FLAME
The most beautiful meditation in the world. ISBN #0-912559-33-0

 THE WELLNESS TAPE
Tap your body's innate ability to renew, heal & revitalize!
ISBN #0-912559-32-2

 TIME TRAVEL
Access your past & future lives. Discover your life's purpose.
ISBN #0-912559-21-7

 YES, I CAN!
Achieve your personal goals & highest potentials.
ISBN #0-912559-09-8

 YOGA NIDRA/ HYPNOYOGA
The ancient Oriental method for advancing to cosmic consciousness.
ISBN #0-912559-34-9

A Gift For Yourself!

Please print your name & address:

Name: _____

Address: _____

City/Zip: _____

Phone: (_____) _____

E-mail Address: _____

A Gift for A Friend!

Make someone happy! Send them a book or tape today!

If the order is for a friend, please print their name, address and any
greeting you wish to send, and we will mail it to them from you!

To:

Name: _____

Friend's Address: _____

City/Zip: _____

Friend's Phone: (_____) _____

Greeting: _____

_____

To order additional gifts for yourself or friends,
feel free to use a separate sheet of paper or xerox this form.

Pay by: ☐ Check   ☐ Money Order   ☐ Credit Card: ☐ | VISA | MasterCard

Name on Credit Card_____

Credit Card # _____

Exp. Date _____

Signature _____

SEND TO:

CREATIVITY UNLIMITED PRESS®

30819 Casilina Drive, Rancho Palos Verdes, CA 90275 U.S.A.
OR CALL: (310) 541-4844

CREATIVITY UNLIMITED PRESS ORDER FORM

(310) 541-4844

Check the boxes of your choice (if more than one, insert quantity)

BOOKS

- ☐ AUTOMATIC WRITING & HIEROSCRIPTING ....$ 9.95
- ☐ COSMIC WELLNESS ....$ 19.95
- ☐ CHANNELING: YOU CONDUIT! ....$ 19.95
- ☐ DENIAL IS NOT A RIVER IN EGYPT: STOCKWELL SYSTEM ....$ 24.95
- ☐ EVERYTHING YOU EVER WANTED TO KNOW ABOUT ....$ 14.95
- ☐ HYPNOSIS: Smile On Your Face & Money In Your Pocket.................$ 19.95
- ☐ INSIDES OUT ....$ 6.95
- ☐ SEX & OTHER TOUCHY SUBJECTS..$ 14.95
- ☐ STOCKWELL'S HYPNOSIS FOR WEIGHT LOSS ....$ 19.95
- ☐ THE SEARCH FOR COSMIC CONSCIOUSNESS ....$ 19.95
- ☐ THE SECRETS OF HYPNOTIZING MEN ....$ 19.95
- ☐ THE SECRETS OF HYPNOTIZING WOMEN...................................$ 19.95
- ☐ TIME TRAVEL: PAST LIFE HANDBOOK ....$ 19.95
- ☐ WEDDING LOVE LETTERS..$ 19.95

SELF HYPNOSIS AUDIO CASSETTES

- ☐ AUTOMATIC WRITING............$10
- ☐ EVERYTHING/10 STEPS SUPER CONS.....$10
- ☐ FLIGHT ATTENDANT WELL-BEING.....$10
- ☐ GREAT GOLF $14.95
- ☐ GREAT TENNIS...................$14.95
- ☐ I LOVE EXERCISE (CD $20) $10
- ☐ KUNDALINI RISING...................$10
- ☐ LOSE WEIGHT.........................$10
- ☐ MER-KA-BA $10
- ☐ MAGNETIC MIND TONING........$10
- ☐ MEET YOUR ANGEL $10

- ☐ NO MORE ALCOHOL.................$10
- ☐ NO MORE SUGAR JUNKIE $10
- ☐ PEACE AND CALM..................$10
- ☐ QUIT SMOKING $10
- ☐ SANDY BEACH MEDITATION $10
- ☐ SLEEP, BEAUTIFUL SLEEP $10
- ☐ THE MONEY TAPE...................$10
- ☐ THE VIOLET FLAME $10
- ☐ THE WELLNESS TAPE $10
- ☐ TIME TRAVEL $10
- ☐ YES! I CAN $10
- ☐ YOGA NIDRA/HYPNOYOGA....$10

CHILDREN'S AUDIO CASSETTES

- ☐ MOMMY BUNNY'S GOING TO WORK $10
- ☐ U R WHAT U EAT $10

MUSIC AND SONG AUDIO CASSETTES

- ☐ DEEP INTO A CALMING OCEAN $10
- ☐ SERENITY RESONANCE SOUND ....AUDIO $10 / CD $25
- ☐ SEX & OTHER TOUCHY SUBJECTS $10

VIDEO

- ☐ HIGHER SELF HYPNOSIS SERIES (all 3 below): ....$ 55.00
- ☐ HYPNOTICALLY YOURS; Ormond McGill $19.95
- ☐ Secret Lives of McGill ☐ Secrets of the Mind ☐ Secrets of Stage Hypnosis each $19.95
- ☐ STATIC GRIT ON MY CB: ☐ Music Video or ☐ Audio Cassette $10.00
- ☐ THE ART OF CHANNELING: ....$ 19.95
- ☐ TRANCEFORMATIONS: Hypnosis, Channeling & Past Life $19.95

BOXED SETS

- ☐ RELEASE WEIGHT BOOK, VIDEO, 4 AUDIO TAPES....................................$85
- ☐ RELEASE WEIGHT SET, INSTRUCTORS VERSION $125

SUBTOTAL

ADD $2.50 POSTAGE & HANDLING PER ITEM
CA residents add 8.25% tax, Foreign countries add an add'l $6.00 per item

TOTAL

A Gift For Yourself!

Please print your name & address:

Name: _____

Address: _____

City/Zip: _____

Phone: (_____) _____

E-mail Address: _____

A Gift for A Friend!

Make someone happy! Send them a book or tape today!

If the order is for a friend, please print their name, address and any greeting you wish to send, and we will mail it to them from you!

To:

Name: _____

Friend's Address: _____

City/Zip: _____

Friend's Phone: (_____) _____

Greeting: _____

_____

To order additional gifts for yourself or friends,
feel free to use a separate sheet of paper or xerox this form.

Pay by: ☐ Check   ☐ Money Order   ☐ Credit Card: [☐] VISA MasterCard

Name on Credit Card_____

Credit Card # _____

Exp. Date _____

Signature _____

<u>**SEND TO:**</u>

 **CREATIVITY UNLIMITED PRESS®**

30819 Casilina Drive, Rancho Palos Verdes, CA 90275 U.S.A.
OR CALL: (310) 541-4844

CREATIVITY UNLIMITED PRESS ORDER FORM

(310) 541-4844

Check the boxes of your choice (if more than one, insert quantity)

BOOKS
- ☐ AUTOMATIC WRITING & HIEROSCRIPTING ....$ 9.95
- ☐ COSMIC WELLNESS ....$ 19.95
- ☐ CHANNELING: YOU CONDUIT!...$ 19.95
- ☐ DENIAL IS NOT A RIVER IN EGYPT: STOCKWELL SYSTEM.....................$ 24.95
- ☐ EVERYTHING YOU EVER WANTED TO KNOW ABOUT ....$ 14.95
- ☐ HYPNOSIS: Smile On Your Face & Money In Your Pocket..................$ 19.95
- ☐ INSIDES OUT ....$ 6.95
- ☐ SEX & OTHER TOUCHY SUBJECTS...$ 14.95
- ☐ STOCKWELL'S HYPNOSIS FOR WEIGHT LOSS ....$ 19.95
- ☐ THE SEARCH FOR COSMIC CONSCIOUSNESS ....$ 19.95
- ☐ THE SECRETS OF HYPNOTIZING MEN ....$ 19.95
- ☐ THE SECRETS OF HYPNOTIZING WOMEN.....................................$ 19.95
- ☐ TIME TRAVEL: PAST LIFE HANDBOOK ....$ 19.95
- ☐ WEDDING LOVE LETTERS..$ 19.95

SELF HYPNOSIS AUDIO CASSETTES
- ☐ AUTOMATIC WRITING.............$10
- ☐ EVERYTHING/10 STEPS SUPER CONS.....$10
- ☐ FLIGHT ATTENDANT WELL-BEING.....$10
- ☐ GREAT GOLF $14.95
- ☐ GREAT TENNIS...................$14.95
- ☐ I LOVE EXERCISE (CD $20) $10
- ☐ KUNDALINI RISING...................$10
- ☐ LOSE WEIGHT.........................$10
- ☐ MER-KA-BA $10
- ☐ MAGNETIC MIND TONING........$10
- ☐ MEET YOUR ANGEL $10
- ☐ NO MORE ALCOHOL.................$10
- ☐ NO MORE SUGAR JUNKIE $10
- ☐ PEACE AND CALM...................$10
- ☐ QUIT SMOKING $10
- ☐ SANDY BEACH MEDITATION $10
- ☐ SLEEP, BEAUTIFUL SLEEP $10
- ☐ THE MONEY TAPE...................$10
- ☐ THE VIOLET FLAME $10
- ☐ THE WELLNESS TAPE $10
- ☐ TIME TRAVEL $10
- ☐ YES! I CAN $10
- ☐ YOGA NIDRA/HYPNOYOGA $10

CHILDREN'S AUDIO CASSETTES
- ☐ MOMMY BUNNY'S GOING TO WORK $10
- ☐ U R WHAT U EAT $10

MUSIC AND SONG AUDIO CASSETTES
- ☐ DEEP INTO A CALMING OCEAN $10
- ☐ SERENITY RESONANCE SOUND ....AUDIO $10 / CD $25
- ☐ SEX & OTHER TOUCHY SUBJECTS $10

VIDEO
- ☐ HIGHER SELF HYPNOSIS SERIES (all 3 below): ....$ 55.00
- ☐ HYPNOTICALLY YOURS; Ormond McGill $19.95
- ☐ Secret Lives of McGill ☐ Secrets of the Mind ☐ Secrets of Stage Hypnosis each $19.95
- ☐ STATIC GRIT ON MY CB: ☐ Music Video or ☐ Audio Cassette $10.00
- ☐ THE ART OF CHANNELING: ....$ 19.95
- ☐ TRANCEFORMATIONS: Hypnosis, Channeling & Past Life $19.95

BOXED SETS
- ☐ RELEASE WEIGHT BOOK, VIDEO, 4 AUDIO TAPES.....................................$85
- ☐ RELEASE WEIGHT SET, INSTRUCTORS VERSION $125

SUBTOTAL

ADD $2.50 POSTAGE & HANDLING PER ITEM
CA residents add 8.25% tax, Foreign countries add an add'l $6.00 per item

TOTAL

A Gift For Yourself!

Please print your name & address:

Name: _____

Address: _____

City/Zip: _____

Phone: (_____) _____

E-mail Address: _____

A Gift for A Friend!

Make someone happy! Send them a book or tape today!

If the order is for a friend, please print their name, address and any
greeting you wish to send, and we will mail it to them from you!

To:

Name: _____

Friend's Address: _____

City/Zip: _____

Friend's Phone: (_____) _____

Greeting: _____

_____

To order additional gifts for yourself or friends,
feel free to use a separate sheet of paper or xerox this form.

Pay by: ☐ Check   ☐ Money Order   ☐ Credit Card: ☐ *VISA* MasterCard

Name on Credit Card_____

Credit Card # _____

Exp. Date _____

Signature _____

CREATIVITY UNLIMITED PRESS ORDER FORM

(310) 541-4844

Check the boxes of your choice (if more than one, insert quantity)

BOOKS
- ☐ AUTOMATIC WRITING & HIEROSCRIPTING .... $ 9.95
- ☐ COSMIC WELLNESS .... $ 19.95
- ☐ CHANNELING: YOU CONDUIT! .... $ 19.95
- ☐ DENIAL IS NOT A RIVER IN EGYPT: STOCKWELL SYSTEM .... $ 24.95
- ☐ EVERYTHING YOU EVER WANTED TO KNOW ABOUT .... $ 14.95
- ☐ HYPNOSIS: Smile On Your Face & Money In Your Pocket .... $ 19.95
- ☐ INSIDES OUT .... $ 6.95
- ☐ SEX & OTHER TOUCHY SUBJECTS .... $ 14.95
- ☐ STOCKWELL'S HYPNOSIS FOR WEIGHT LOSS .... $ 19.95
- ☐ THE SEARCH FOR COSMIC CONSCIOUSNESS .... $ 19.95
- ☐ THE SECRETS OF HYPNOTIZING MEN .... $ 19.95
- ☐ THE SECRETS OF HYPNOTIZING WOMEN .... $ 19.95
- ☐ TIME TRAVEL: PAST LIFE HANDBOOK .... $ 19.95
- ☐ WEDDING LOVE LETTERS .... $ 19.95

SELF HYPNOSIS AUDIO CASSETTES
- ☐ AUTOMATIC WRITING $10
- ☐ EVERYTHING/10 STEPS SUPER CONS..... $10
- ☐ FLIGHT ATTENDANT WELL-BEING..... $10
- ☐ GREAT GOLF $14.95
- ☐ GREAT TENNIS $14.95
- ☐ I LOVE EXERCISE (CD $20) $10
- ☐ KUNDALINI RISING $10
- ☐ LOSE WEIGHT $10
- ☐ MER-KA-BA $10
- ☐ MAGNETIC MIND TONING $10
- ☐ MEET YOUR ANGEL $10
- ☐ NO MORE ALCOHOL $10
- ☐ NO MORE SUGAR JUNKIE $10
- ☐ PEACE AND CALM $10
- ☐ QUIT SMOKING $10
- ☐ SANDY BEACH MEDITATION $10
- ☐ SLEEP, BEAUTIFUL SLEEP $10
- ☐ THE MONEY TAPE $10
- ☐ THE VIOLET FLAME $10
- ☐ THE WELLNESS TAPE $10
- ☐ TIME TRAVEL $10
- ☐ YES! I CAN $10
- ☐ YOGA NIDRA/HYPNOYOGA $10

CHILDREN'S AUDIO CASSETTES
- ☐ MOMMY BUNNY'S GOING TO WORK $10
- ☐ U R WHAT U EAT $10

MUSIC AND SONG AUDIO CASSETTES
- ☐ DEEP INTO A CALMING OCEAN $10
- ☐ SERENITY RESONANCE SOUND .... AUDIO $10 / CD $25
- ☐ SEX & OTHER TOUCHY SUBJECTS $10

VIDEO
- ☐ HIGHER SELF HYPNOSIS SERIES (all 3 below): .... $ 55.00
- ☐ HYPNOTICALLY YOURS; Ormond McGill $19.95
- ☐ Secret Lives of McGill ☐ Secrets of the Mind ☐ Secrets of Stage Hypnosis each $19.95
- ☐ STATIC GRIT ON MY CB: ☐ Music Video or ☐ Audio Cassette $10.00
- ☐ THE ART OF CHANNELING .... $ 19.95
- ☐ TRANCEFORMATIONS: Hypnosis, Channeling & Past Life $19.95

BOXED SETS
- ☐ RELEASE WEIGHT BOOK, VIDEO, 4 AUDIO TAPES $85
- ☐ RELEASE WEIGHT SET, INSTRUCTORS VERSION $125

SUBTOTAL

ADD $2.50 POSTAGE & HANDLING PER ITEM
CA residents add 8.25% tax, Foreign countries add an add'l $6.00 per item

TOTAL

A Gift For Yourself!

Please print your name & address:

Name: _____

Address: _____

City/Zip: _____

Phone: (_____) _____

E-mail Address: _____

A Gift for A Friend!

Make someone happy! Send them a book or tape today!

If the order is for a friend, please print their name, address and any greeting you wish to send, and we will mail it to them from you!

To:

Name: _____

Friend's Address: _____

City/Zip: _____

Friend's Phone: (_____) _____

Greeting: _____

_____

To order additional gifts for yourself or friends,
feel free to use a separate sheet of paper or xerox this form.

Pay by: ☐ Check   ☐ Money Order   ☐ Credit Card: [⚫ | VISA | MasterCard]

Name on Credit Card_____

Credit Card # _____

Exp. Date _____

Signature _____

CREATIVITY UNLIMITED PRESS ORDER FORM

(310) 541-4844

Check the boxes of your choice (if more than one, insert quantity)

BOOKS

- ☐ AUTOMATIC WRITING & HIEROSCRIPTING ....$ 9.95
- ☐ COSMIC WELLNESS ....$ 19.95
- ☐ CHANNELING: YOU CONDUIT! ....$ 19.95
- ☐ DENIAL IS NOT A RIVER IN EGYPT: STOCKWELL SYSTEM ....$ 24.95
- ☐ EVERYTHING YOU EVER WANTED TO KNOW ABOUT ....$ 14.95
- ☐ HYPNOSIS: Smile On Your Face & Money In Your Pocket..................$ 19.95
- ☐ INSIDES OUT ....$ 6.95
- ☐ SEX & OTHER TOUCHY SUBJECTS...$ 14.95
- ☐ STOCKWELL'S HYPNOSIS FOR WEIGHT LOSS ....$ 19.95
- ☐ THE SEARCH FOR COSMIC CONSCIOUSNESS ....$ 19.95
- ☐ THE SECRETS OF HYPNOTIZING MEN ....$ 19.95
- ☐ THE SECRETS OF HYPNOTIZING WOMEN...$ 19.95
- ☐ TIME TRAVEL: PAST LIFE HANDBOOK ....$ 19.95
- ☐ WEDDING LOVE LETTERS..$ 19.95

SELF HYPNOSIS AUDIO CASSETTES

- ☐ AUTOMATIC WRITING.............$10
- ☐ EVERYTHING/10 STEPS SUPER CONS.....$10
- ☐ FLIGHT ATTENDANT WELL-BEING.....$10
- ☐ GREAT GOLF $14.95
- ☐ GREAT TENNIS....................$14.95
- ☐ I LOVE EXERCISE (CD $20) $10
- ☐ KUNDALINI RISING...................$10
- ☐ LOSE WEIGHT.........................$10
- ☐ MER-KA-BA $10
- ☐ MAGNETIC MIND TONING........$10
- ☐ MEET YOUR ANGEL $10
- ☐ NO MORE ALCOHOL.................$10
- ☐ NO MORE SUGAR JUNKIE $10
- ☐ PEACE AND CALM...................$10
- ☐ QUIT SMOKING $10
- ☐ SANDY BEACH MEDITATION $10
- ☐ SLEEP, BEAUTIFUL SLEEP $10
- ☐ THE MONEY TAPE....................$10
- ☐ THE VIOLET FLAME $10
- ☐ THE WELLNESS TAPE $10
- ☐ TIME TRAVEL $10
- ☐ YES! I CAN $10
- ☐ YOGA NIDRA/HYPNOYOGA $10

CHILDREN'S AUDIO CASSETTES

- ☐ MOMMY BUNNY'S GOING TO WORK $10
- ☐ U R WHAT U EAT $10

MUSIC AND SONG AUDIO CASSETTES

- ☐ DEEP INTO A CALMING OCEAN $10
- ☐ SERENITY RESONANCE SOUND ....AUDIO $10 / CD $25
- ☐ SEX & OTHER TOUCHY SUBJECTS $10

VIDEO

- ☐ HIGHER SELF HYPNOSIS SERIES (all 3 below): ....$ 55.00
- ☐ HYPNOTICALLY YOURS; Ormond McGill $19.95
- ☐ Secret Lives of McGill ☐ Secrets of Stage Hypnosis each $19.95
- ☐ STATIC GRIT ON MY CB: ☐ Music Video or ☐ Audio Cassette $10.00
- ☐ THE ART OF CHANNELING: ....$ 19.95
- ☐ TRANCEFORMATIONS: Hypnosis, Channeling & Past LIfe $19.95

BOXED SETS

- ☐ RELEASE WEIGHT BOOK, VIDEO, 4 AUDIO TAPES....................................$85
- ☐ RELEASE WEIGHT SET, INSTRUCTORS VERSION $125

SUBTOTAL

ADD $2.50 POSTAGE & HANDLING PER ITEM
CA residents add 8.25% tax, Foreign countries add an add'l $6.00 per item

TOTAL